TREES
TO KNOW IN
OREGON

EC 1450
Revised June 2003

Authors
Edward C. Jensen, professor, College of Forestry,
Oregon State University
—and—
Charles R. Ross, Extension forester emeritus,
Oregon State University

"Oregon's Forests" by
Ralph E. Duddles, Extension forester emeritus, Coos and Curry counties,
and Allan Campbell III, Extension forester emeritus, Jackson County;
Oregon State University
—and—
Lou Torres, former public affairs specialist,
Oregon Department of Forestry

Principal Artist
Hugh J. Hayes
Oregon Department of Forestry, retired

Photographer
Edward C. Jensen

Publisher
Oregon State University Extension Service

ISBN 1-931979-03-0

Contents

Don't Go into the Woods
—before learning to identify this!

poisonoak (Rhus diversiloba)

Poisonoak is not really an oak; therefore, its common name is correctly written either as one word rather than two (poisonoak) or hyphenated (poison-oak).

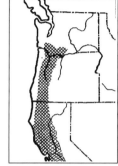

Habit: Grows as a trailing or climbing vine, or as an upright shrub.

Leaves: Pinnately compound (usually in threes), deciduous, and alternate. Wavy margins with irregular lobes. Size of leaflets varies dramatically (2–6" long).

Twigs: Slender, tan. May have grasping tendrils. Have naked buds.

Flowers and fruit: Flowers are small, clustered, and inconspicuous. Fruits are small white drupes with fine, black lines.

Itch, itch, itch. Poisonoak gives most people an itchy rash when they touch it. All parts of the plant—leaves, stems, flowers, fruits, and roots—contain an irritating chemical, so no part is safe to touch. And because the chemical is present all year, you must always be careful around poisonoak. Many people are so allergic to poisonoak that they develop a rash after handling a pet who has walked through a patch of it, and some even get it from the smoke of burning plants.

Leaves of three—let it be. Poisonoak leaves are pinnately compound with three leaflets per leaf, but leaflets may range dramatically in size and shape. When growing in sun, they are commonly 2 to 3 inches long, but in shade they may reach 6 inches long. Margins are wavy and irregularly lobed, often with several lobes on one edge and no lobes on another. Their leaves turn beautiful reds and yellows in the fall. Poisonoak has three diverse growth forms: it can grow as an upright shrub, crawl along the ground, or climb high into trees, sending down long, thin branches to "catch" those passing by.

Range. Poisonoak grows primarily at low elevations on the west side of the Cascades from southern British Columbia through southern California. It grows in both the sun and the shade, but is especially fond of dry places.

Folklore about poisonoak. Folklore has it that eating a poisonoak leaf when you're young will make you resistant to its toxin. DON'T BELIEVE IT—you're likely to end up with a terrible rash! Some people seem to have a natural immunity to poisonoak, but most don't. Also, immunity may change with age and exposure to the chemical. Your best protection is to learn to recognize poisonoak and then to protect yourself from it, either by wearing long clothing or by avoiding it altogether.

How to Identify Trees

Tree Detective

Identifying trees is a lot like identifying people. You can easily recognize a close friend, even if you catch only a glimpse. In fact, you can often recognize a friend from a fast-moving car, or even from a picture in a photo album when the friend was a very different age or had a different appearance. However, if you meet a room full of strangers, you need to concentrate on individual characteristics before you can begin to tell them apart. And even then you might struggle to get their names right!

It's the same with trees. When you know a tree well, you'll be able to name it whether you see its leaves, its fruit, its flowers, or even its shape and color. When you know it well enough, you'll be able to recognize it in different stages of growth, in different locations, and even from fast-moving cars! You may even want to learn its formal or scientific name, which is written in Latin.

How can you get to know trees that well? First, learn to identify their leaves, flowers, and fruit. Then, as you become better friends, examine each tree more carefully. Look at its bark, its branching pattern, its color, and its shape. Eventually, you may even get to know many trees by where they live.

This book can help you start to know Oregon's trees. Keep it handy—you'll be surprised how easy and fun tree identification can be!

Name That Tree

Tree names can be very confusing until you understand how they're developed. All plants have two names: a **common name** and a **scientific name.** Common names are written in English (or in German if you're in Germany, or in French if you're in France), but scientific names always are written in Latin, so they can be used anywhere in the world.

In addition, most trees have two-part common names and two-part scientific names. One part of each name refers to the general type of tree (like "larch" in western larch), while the other refers to the specific type of larch (like "western" in western larch). In this case, larch is the **genus** and western is the **species.** In the scientific name, the order is reversed—the genus name comes first and the species name comes second. Therefore, the Latin name of western larch is *Larix occidentalis,* where *Larix* indicates the genus and *occidentalis* indicates the species.

For example:

western larch: *Larix occidentalis*

Name	Genus	Species
Common	larch	western
Scientific	*Larix*	*occidentalis*

Other larches have the same genus name in both English and Latin, but they have different species names. For example:

subalpine larch: *Larix lyallii*
eastern larch: *Larix laricina*

Although this naming system takes a while to get used to, you'll soon realize that learning tree names can be fun. They often tell you something special about the tree—such as who discovered it, a particular growth characteristic, or where it grows. When you encounter a new plant, see what you can learn from its name.

Tree Terms

Trees are woody plants that typically have one main stem, called a trunk, and are over 20 feet tall at maturity. Shrubs, on the other hand, are woody plants that typically have multiple stems and are less than 20 feet tall at maturity. Although there are exceptions to this, it's a good rule of thumb.

Oregon's trees fit into two major categories: conifers and broadleaves. **Conifers** have needlelike or scalelike leaves and usually bear seeds inside woody cones. Conifers are often called **evergreens** because most hold their leaves all year long; however, some conifers are deciduous—they drop their leaves in winter. All conifers are also called **softwoods** because their wood is relatively soft when compared with that of other trees. Broadleaved trees, or **broadleaves**, usually have wide, flat leaves and bear their seeds inside soft fruits. All broadleaved trees are referred to as **hardwoods** because their wood generally is harder than that of conifers. A few, however, like cottonwoods and balsa, have very soft wood. Most broadleaved trees are **deciduous** —that is, they drop their leaves in winter—but a few are evergreen.

The following diagram may help you understand the relationship between these terms.

Thousands of terms are used to describe trees. Luckily, we need only a few to begin identifying trees successfully.

Trees and Groups of Trees

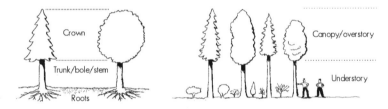

Leaf and Branching Patterns

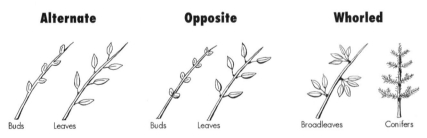

Leaf Types and Arrangements

Broadleaves

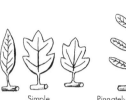

Simple

Pinnately compound

Palmately compound

Conifers

Spirally arranged

Two-ranked

Clusters/bundles/fascilles

Massed

Parts of a Leaf

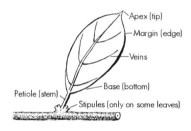

Apex (tip)

Margin (edge)

Veins

Base (bottom)

Petiole (stem)

Stipules (only on some leaves)

Leaf Shapes

Broadleaves

Lance-shaped
(Lanceolate)

Egg-shaped
(Ovate)

Reverse
egg-shaped
(Obovate)

Elliptical/
oblong

Conifers

Needle-like

Linear

Scale-like

Awl-like

Leaf Margins

Entire

Wavy

Serrate

Doubly serrate

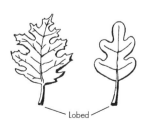

Lobed

Leaf Tips and Bases

Tips

Acute
(pointed)

Rounded
(blunt)

Notched

Truncated
(cut off)

Bases

Asymmetrical
(uneven)

Truncated
(cut off)

Leaf Veins

Pinnate

Arcuate
(curved)

Palmate

Fruits

Cones

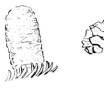

Dry Fruits

Single
samara

Double samara

Legume

Acorn

Nut

Fleshy Fruits

Drupe
(1 seed)

Berry
(many seeds)

Pome (apple, pear)

Twigs

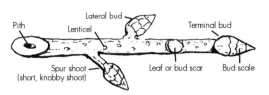

Pith

Lateral bud

Lenticel

Terminal bud

Spur shoot
(short, knobby shoot)

Leaf or bud scar

Bud scale

The Key to Successful Identification

Fortunately, we don't need to remember *all* the characteristics of every tree. **Keys** help us make the most important distinctions. Keys come in all shapes and sizes. Some are based on pictures and some are based on words; some cover only trees while others cover only wildflowers; some are simple to use and some are very difficult. Most help us divide plants into two groups—those that have a particular characteristic and those that don't have it. If any group of plants is split often enough, eventually there will be only one plant left. If the key is accurate, and if we've made good decisions along the way, we'll have correctly identified the plant.

Using a key is like following the branches of a tree—each additional branch gets smaller and smaller until you reach a single branch tip. All the species described in a key are represented by the trunk, while each branch tip represents a single species of tree.

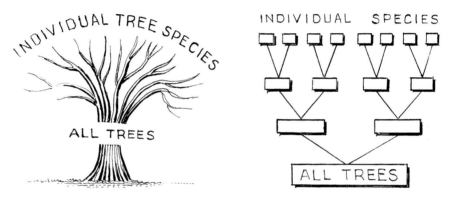

This book contains two keys, one for conifers (on page 11) and one for broadleaved trees (on page 59). They work exactly the same way, although the broadleaf key is longer because it contains more trees. To identify a plant using the keys in this book, first decide whether the tree you want to identify is a conifer or a broadleaf. Then turn to the appropriate key.

Oregon's Native Conifers

Oregon's diverse topography and climate combine to create a variety of habitats in which conifers thrive. Nearly 30 species of conifers are native to Oregon. Though most have leaves shaped like needles, a few have leaves shaped like scales.

Conifers grow especially well on the west slopes of the Cascades and throughout the Coast Range, where relatively warm temperatures and abundant rainfall allow them to grow even in winter. Conifers also grow well on the east side of the Cascades because their needlelike leaves have small surface areas and thick, waxy coverings that help the trees retain moisture during the hot, dry summers and cold, dry winters. And conifers grow well at high elevations because their evergreen nature allows them to begin growing in the spring as soon as temperatures rise above freezing.

Oregon's conifers can be grouped into 12 different genera based on the structure of their "flowers" and fruit. The genera with needlelike leaves include: Douglas-fir, pine, fir, spruce, larch, hemlock, redwood, and yew. Those with scalelike leaves include: arborvitae (sometimes called redcedar), incense-cedar, white-cedar (including Port-Orford-cedar and Alaska-cedar), and juniper.

To identify Oregon's native conifers, turn to the key on the next page. To learn more about the forests that these trees compose, turn to the section of this book called "Oregon's Forests" (page 114).

To Use This Key

1. Start at the top of the key. Then read each of the two statements listed directly below the starting point.

2. Decide which of the two statements better describes the plant you're trying to identify. Then read the two statements directly under that box.

3. Continue this process until you've identified a single group of trees (called a genus). Then turn to the page indicated and read the descriptions of individual species contained within that genus (there may be only one, or there may be several).

4. If the species description matches the plant you're trying to identify—GREAT! If it doesn't match, go back to the beginning of the key and try again.

Remember, identifying trees is a bit like detective work—sometimes you need to follow false leads to discover the truth eventually.

Common Conifers of Oregon

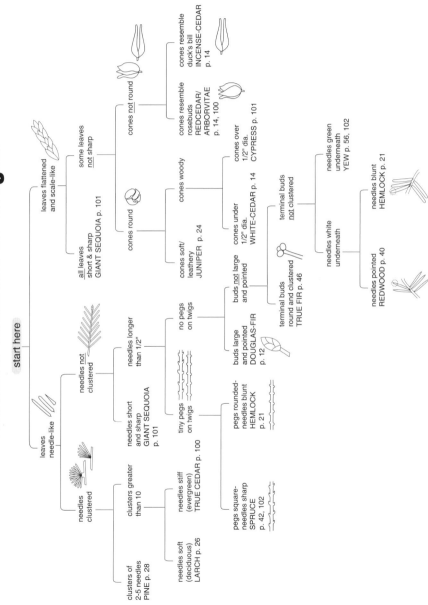

start here

leaves needle-like

- **needles clustered**
  - **clusters greater than 10**
    - **needles soft (deciduous)** LARCH p. 26
    - **needles stiff (evergreen)** TRUE CEDAR p. 100
  - **clusters of 2-5 needles** PINE p. 28

- **needles not clustered**
  - **needles short and sharp** GIANT SEQUOIA p. 101
  - **needles longer than 1/2"**
    - **tiny pegs on twigs**
      - **pegs square-needles sharp** SPRUCE p. 42, 102
      - **pegs rounded-needles blunt** HEMLOCK p. 21
    - **no pegs on twigs**
      - **buds large and pointed** DOUGLAS-FIR p. 12
      - **buds not large and pointed**
        - **terminal buds round and clustered** TRUE FIR p. 46
        - **terminal buds not clustered**
          - **needles white underneath**
            - **needles pointed** REDWOOD p. 40
            - **needles blunt** HEMLOCK p. 21
          - **needles green underneath** YEW p. 56, 102

leaves flattened and scale-like

- **all leaves short & sharp** GIANT SEQUOIA p. 101
- **some leaves not sharp**
  - **cones round**
    - **cones soft/leathery** JUNIPER p. 24
    - **cones woody**
      - **cones under 1/2" dia.** WHITE-CEDAR p. 14
      - **cones over 1/2" dia.** CYPRESS p. 101
  - **cones not round**
    - **cones resemble rosebuds** REDCEDAR/ARBORVITAE p. 14, 100
    - **cones resemble duck's bill** INCENSE-CEDAR p. 14

Douglas-firs *(Pseudotsuga)*

Douglas-fir is the name of an entire genus of trees that contains six species—two native to North America and four native to eastern Asia. Because of its similarity to other genera, Douglas-fir has given botanists fits. It has, at various times, been called a pine, a spruce, a hemlock, and a true fir. In 1867, because of its distinctive cones, it was given its own genus—*Pseudotsuga*—which means false hemlock. The hyphen in the common name lets us know that Douglas-fir is not a "true" fir—that it's not a member of the *Abies* genus.

Only one Douglas-fir is native to Oregon, and it's by far the most important member of the entire genus. Its common name is identical to that of the genus, reflecting its importance.

Douglas-fir *(Pseudotsuga menziesii)*

Size: Full-grown trees may exceed 250' in height and 10' in diameter. In 1994, the world's largest Douglas-fir grew in Coos County, Oregon; it stood 330' tall and was over 11' in diameter.

Needles: About 1" long with a blunt tip. Spirally arranged, but may be two-ranked in the shade. Green above with two white bands underneath.

Fruit: Woody cone 3–4" long; pitchfork-shaped bracts are longer than scales. Hang down.

Twigs: Large, pointed buds with reddish-brown, overlapping scales. Small, round, partially raised leaf scars.

Bark: Has resin blisters when young; deeply furrowed and reddish-brown when mature.

 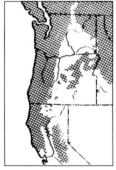

Oregon's most common tree. West of the Cascades, you could guess that any needle-leaved tree in the forest is a Douglas-fir and be right 8 out of 10 times. Douglas-fir also is common east of the Cascades, especially at mid to high elevations. Douglas-fir is Oregon's state tree.

The cone everybody knows. Put a Douglas-fir cone among all cones of the Northwest and it stands out. Only Douglas-fir has three-pointed bracts sticking out between the cone scales like little tongues. These bracts have been compared to a three-pronged pitchfork and to the hind feet and tail of a mouse diving into a hole. Cones are almost always present, either on the trees or under them. Even young saplings often have them.

Other clues to identification. The buds of Douglas-fir also help identify it. They're sharp-pointed, have reddish-brown overlapping scales, and shine like a highly polished shoe. The needles usually surround the twig like the bristles of a bottle brush and are soft to touch. Cut bark reveals two layers of color that look like bacon (alternating layers of red and cream). Stands of Douglas-fir are striking from a distance because of the uniform angles of their limbs.

Bracts identify Douglas-fir

A special name. This tree's name reflects the uncertainty that surrounded it for so many years and, at the same time, honors two of the outstanding naturalists of all time. The common name, Douglas-fir, is hyphenated to show that it's not really a fir, while the scientific name, *Pseudotsuga*, means "false hemlock." The "Douglas" in the common name honors David Douglas, a young Scottish botanist who roamed the Northwest in the 1820s while working for the Royal Horti-culture Society of England. The "*menziesii*" in the scientific name honors Archibald Menzies, the Scottish physician and naturalist who discovered the tree on Vancouver Island in 1791 while serving in the British Navy.

Sharp-pointed buds

Tree of 1,000 uses. Douglas-fir trees are tremendously important to Oregon and the nation. They furnish more products for human use than any other tree in the world. They can be fashioned into poles and beams hundreds of feet long or can be broken into microscopic fibers for making paper. Lumber and plywood from Douglas-fir are used to build houses, farms, factories, bridges, docks, furniture, and boats. Resin from its bark is used to make glues and photographic supplies. Shredded bark is a popular mulch under trees and shrubs in home landscapes. Douglas-fir forests are home to a wide array of wildlife: thundering herds of elk; secretive bob-cats, cougars, bears, and deer; and a tremendous variety of birds, insects, and small mammals. The soil in Douglas-fir forests is rich in nutrients and soil organisms and plays a vital role in filtering Oregon's water supply. Oregon's Douglas-fir forests are also among the nation's most heavily used forests for recreation, and Douglas-fir is the nation's most popular Christmas tree.

Leads in lumber and plywood

Fire—friend and foe. Fire is both a friend and foe to Douglas-fir, depending on the size of the trees and the size of the fire. Large Douglas-firs have very thick bark that can resist the heat of all but the hottest fires. Therefore, in an older forest, small fires simply clear competing vegetation from around larger Douglas-firs. Because Douglas-fir seeds need to germinate on bare mineral soil, they often seed-in following fires that consume the needles, branches, and green plants that typically occupy the forest floor. Large, cata-strophic fires, however, kill trees both large and small. Many of the vast stands of old-growth Douglas-fir that currently occupy western Oregon and Washington owe their existence to huge fires that swept through the Northwest 400 to 600 years ago.

1904, Portland: First commercial plywood panels made

Eastside Douglas-fir. East of the Cascade summit, Douglas-fir is a smaller tree. In addition, its cones are shorter and have stiffer bracts. This eastside variety is sometimes called Rocky Mountain Douglas-fir, and it ranges from Canada to Mexico.

False Cedars *(Calocedrus, Thuja, Chamaecyparis)*

Common names can be confusing—and that is certainly the case with this group of trees. Oregon has four species of trees that are called cedars, but none of them is truly a cedar. In fact, they don't even resemble true cedars. True cedars belong to the genus *Cedrus* (a member of the Pine family) and bear their evergreen needles in dense clusters on small, woody spur shoots. Their cones are large, sit upright on their branches, and fall apart when the seeds are ripe. True cedars are native only to the Mediterranean and Himalayan regions of the world.

Oregon's false cedars have tiny, scalelike foliage and small cones that remain on the tree long after their seeds are gone. Why then are they called "cedars"? Although we can't be sure, it's probably because of their wood. In ancient Rome, *Cedrus* referred to a group of trees with fragrant wood. Our "cedars" also have aromatic wood, and that's probably how the confusion in names first started.

It's easy to recognize our false cedars as a group, but it's more difficult to tell one from another. Their tiny, scalelike leaves overlap like shingles and form flat sprays like a fern. Some have distinctive patterns of white bloom on their undersides; others don't. To make things even more complex, the four separate species fall into three different genera. Cones are often the best way to tell them apart.

All false cedars have scalelike foliage, although each differs slightly. Oregon's four species fall into three genera, but unfortunately their names often are confusing.

Incense-cedar falls into the genus *Calocedrus*, which is called the incense-cedar genus. All incense-cedars have cones shaped like a duck's bill when closed, and a flying goose when open.

Western redcedar falls into the genus *Thuja*, which is commonly called the arborvitae genus. All arborvitae have cones shaped like tiny rose buds, or the bowl of a smoker's pipe.

Port-Orford-cedar and **Alaska-cedar** fall into the genus *Chamaecyparis*, which is commonly called the white-cedar or false cypress genus. All members of this genus have small, round, woody cones.

incense-cedar *(Calocedrus decurrens)*

(formerly called *Libocedrus decurrens*)

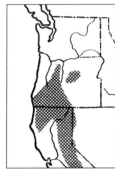

Size: Grows to 110' tall and 5' in diameter.

Needles: Scalelike and appressed to twig; set of four leaves is much longer than it is wide (and is shaped like long-stemmed wine glass); little or no white pattern on underside.

Fruit: Woody cones about 1" long; unopened cones are shaped like a duck's bill; open cones are shaped like a flying goose.

Bark: Flaky when young; platy, furrowed, and reddish-brown when mature.

A false cedar. Like the other false cedars, incense-cedar has scalelike leaves. However, they are much longer than they are wide (other false cedars have leaves just about as wide as they are long). Many say a set of four small scales resembles a long-stemmed wine glass. The cones of incense-cedar are also much different from those of other "cedars"; when open, they look like a flying goose or like Donald Duck's bill with his tongue sticking out. The hyphen in the common name tells you this is not a true cedar.

Rumpled appearance. Branches of mature incense-cedars have a twisted, rumpled appearance, while young trees growing in the open form perfect pyramids. John Muir, one of America's most famous early naturalists, observed that the dense, matted foliage of vigorously growing incense-cedars made a fine shelter from storms. Incense-cedar is a good ornamental or windbreak tree, especially in drier parts of the state. It's fast-growing, attractive, and trouble-free.

Pencil wood. Incense-cedar has aromatic wood that resists insects and decay. However, much wood that otherwise would make quality lumber is riddled by a white fungus called "pencil rot" or "peck." As a result, it seldom finds its way into decking, siding, or shingles. However, its wood is soft, pliable, and easy to machine without splintering—properties that make it one of the few woods in the world suitable for making pencils. In fact, most of the world's supply of wooden pencils once came from southern Oregon. Although incense-cedars are not often used for Christmas trees, the yellow pollen cones that develop midwinter make the branches popular for wreaths and swags.

Where it grows. Although incense-cedar grows throughout most of the Oregon Cascades, it is increasingly common south of Santiam Pass. It is a principal tree in California's forests because it is well adapted to droughty conditions and extreme temperatures.

Scaly leaves look knobby jointed

western redcedar *(Thuja plicata)*

Size: Grows to 200' tall and 10' or more in diameter. Often have swollen, fluted trunks.

Needles: Scalelike and appressed to twig. Green above and a white butterfly pattern below.

Fruit: Small woody cones about ½" long; grow upright on twig. Shaped like tiny rose buds or the bowl of a smoker's pipe.

Bark: Thin, reddish-brown, and stringy.

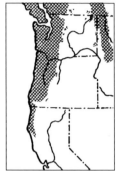

Only native cedar with erect cones

To know western redcedar. Cones and foliage both provide good clues for identifying western redcedar. This is the only native "cedar" with cones turned up and bent backward on the branch. Before opening, they look like the bowl of a smoker's pipe; after opening, they look like tiny rose buds. If you look closely at the underside of the foliage, you can often see a tiny butterfly outlined in white, although some people think it looks more like a bow-tie. The growth form of western redcedar is also a good clue to its identity. The dense, frondlike branches look as if they could shed rain; in fact, some Northwest Indians called this tree "shabalup," which means "dry underneath."

The name game. The genus name, *Thuja*, comes from an ancient Greek word for a highly prized aromatic wood. The species name, *plicata*, means folded into plaits (interwoven); it was probably suggested by the flattened twigs and the fine, regular arrangement of the scalelike leaves. Or, it could come from the long, stringy bark from which fibrous strips are easily pulled. The common name, redcedar, is written as one word to indicate that it's not a true cedar.

Where it grows. Western redcedar grows from Alaska to northern California and from the Pacific Ocean to Montana. It typically grows in moist habitats but occasionally is found on dry slopes. Its commercial range is really the coastal fog belt; damper western Washington and Canada have far greater numbers of these trees than Oregon. The swollen bases of western redcedar make it the broadest of northwest trees—sometimes surpassing 20 feet in diameter!

What it's used for. One of the lightest of coniferous woods, western redcedar is soft in texture, even- and straight-grained, highly attractive, and pleasant to smell. Since the heartwood resists decay, it's prized for uses where it will be exposed to the weather. Unfortunately, old-growth trees that made redcedar's reputation are becoming scarce, and the upcoming second growth is less resistant to insects and decay.

Nevertheless, forest managers welcome the persistent natural regeneration that assures future supplies of this legendary species. Always the leader in shingles and siding, redcedar has other important uses such as poles, posts, pilings, fencing, greenhouse equipment, boats, and outdoor decks.

Redcedar and salmon—mainstays of Northwest Indians. In days gone by, salmon crowded Northwest rivers to assure freedom from hunger, while western redcedar, growing conveniently nearby, supplied material for building lodges and boats, tools and utensils, and a hundred other uses. Strips of bark were fashioned into clothes, baskets, ropes, and fishing nets. For each Northwest Indian relic of stone we find, there once were innumerable articles of wood and bark.

Greatest tree to
Northwest Indians

Northwest Indian housing. Houses or lodges often were made of planks split from western redcedar. Typical lodges were about 20 feet wide and 40 feet long. Boards averaged 2 inches thick and 2 feet wide, although some were as wide as 5 feet. Boards were split from fallen trees with elk horn wedges and stone hammers, then shaped and smoothed with stone tools. Several families occupied a single lodge, each one's space marked by board partitions. Holes in the roof allowed smoke to escape—or at least some of it. Redcedar bark sometimes was used for walls of houses.

Northwest Indian transportation. Redcedar canoes were made by the thousands. A single tree was felled, cut to the desired length, and hollowed out, using a combination of fire and tools made from stone and animal bone. Next it was filled with water into which hot stones were dropped, causing the water to boil and soften the wood so the sides could be spread and curved to the proper form. Abrasive stones that were used to smooth the sides of canoes (and other wood articles) are still found at old dwelling sites. Around 1900, Captain J.C. Voss purchased an ordinary 38-foot dugout cedar canoe from Vancouver Island Indians. Adding a cabin and three small masts, he sailed it 40,000 miles to circumnavigate the globe. Should you visit Victoria, see this canoe at Thunderbird Park.

The fiber of life. Northwest Indians used the inner bark of western redcedar to make blankets, skirts, nets, ropes, mats, baskets, shawls, and other necessities of home and livelihood. Easily worked redcedar wood was a favorite for implements such as arrow and spear shafts, bowls, spoons, and handles, as well as for toys and art work. Bark fibers twisted into ropes were used to lash house timbers together, taking the place of nails. North of Puget Sound, along the coast and its many islands, Northwest Indian craftsmen carved striking designs on redcedar totem poles. Ravens, thunderbirds, bears, wolves, frogs, beavers, salmon, and other animals were often carved in humanlike forms to help explain the intricate relationships between humans and the world around them.

Port-Orford-cedar *(Chamaecyparis lawsoniana)*

Size: Grows to 200' tall and 6' in diameter.

Needles: Scalelike and appressed to the twig. Undersides bear a distinct, white "X" pattern.

Fruit: Small, round, woody cones.

Bark: Brown, fibrous, and ridged. Thicker than the bark of other false cedars.

Tiny white crosses

Popular evergreen ornamental trees

Another false cedar. Port-Orford-cedar looks a lot like western redcedar—except that Port-Orford-cedar has round cones rather than rosebud-shaped cones, and Port-Orford-cedar has white X's, rather than butterflies, underneath its needles. Again, the hyphens in the name tell us that this is not a true cedar.

Small range. The native range of Port-Orford-cedar is very small—a coastal belt stretching 200 miles south from Coos Bay and less than 50 miles inland. In spite of this, it's a familiar tree throughout western Oregon where so many have been planted either as ornamentals for their beautiful shape or for windbreaks because of their uniform growth and dense foliage. Nurseries often incorrectly call Port-Orford-cedars "cypresses" and have developed numerous varieties from the forest species.

Root rot causes concern. In the mid-1900s, a root rot known as *Phytophthora* became a serious killer of Port-Orford-cedar throughout its range. *Phytophthora* is a waterborne disease and under normal conditions spreads slowly. However, it's also picked up by car and truck tires and is spread rapidly by logging trucks and recreational vehicles. Few trees that lie in its path escape alive. Nevertheless, Port-Orford-cedar is so beautiful that many people still risk planting it. If you decide to plant it, select a site where the soil is well drained and won't be disturbed.

Valuable wood. Years ago, the Japanese fell in love with the wood of Port-Orford-cedar because its light color and straight grain reminded them of their sacred Hinoki, a close relative of Port-Orford-cedar. Their heavy buying and the small supply of trees make the better logs very high in price. The wood of Port-Orford-cedar is durable, easy to work, aromatic, and pleasingly textured. Locally it's used similarly to western redcedar. Although archers once used it for arrow shafts, they now rely principally on fiberglass and aluminum alloys. Boughs are very popular in floral displays and commonly are shipped around the world for this purpose.

The future. While Port-Orford-cedar's future is uncertain, scientists are hopeful that nature's evolutionary process of building disease-resistant strains will enable the species to survive. Individual trees that are naturally resistant to *Phytophthora* are found in the forest; perhaps artificial propagation can increase their numbers.

Alaska-cedar *(Chamaecyparis nootkatensis)*

Size: Grows to 100' tall and 4' in diameter, but usually is smaller.

Needles: Scalelike and appressed to twig, but with flaring tips. No white pattern on underside.

Fruit: Small, round, woody cones similar to Port-Orford-cedar's.

Bark: Gray and stringy; often pulling away from tree.

Form: Droopy, weeping appearance.

Similar to Port-Orford-cedar. Alaska-cedar is a close relative of Port-Orford-cedar, but it's easy to tell them apart. Unlike Port-Orford-cedars, there are no white X's on the underside of Alaska-cedar needles. In addition, they grow in very different habitats. In Oregon, Alaska-cedar grows only in cold, wet spots near treeline in the Cascades, and almost always north of Mt. Jefferson. Roundish cones and foliage that's prickly to touch are other details that help distinguish Alaska-cedar from other false cedars likely to be near. Long, drooping sprays give the tree a pronounced weeping appearance and cause many people to think that the tree is dying. When wet, its wood is said to smell like a moldy potato. The scientific name *nootkatensis* commemorates the place it was first seen by Europeans, Nootka Sound on Vancouver Island.

Uses. While the wood of Alaska-cedar is very resistant to insects and decay and is of good commercial quality, the tree is so scarce in Oregon that it has little commercial value here. However, in Canada and coastal Alaska, it's very

Rough, scaly bark

valuable. The sweet-smelling wood is very durable, is easily worked, and can be finished beautifully. It's especially attractive in window frames and exterior doors and finds many uses in boat construction. Indians of southeast Alaska carved canoe paddles and ceremonial masks from this wood. Like Port-Orford-cedar, Alaska-cedar often is exported to Japan. Alaska-cedar also is prized for ornamental purposes because of its beautiful weeping growth form. Another common name for this tree is Alaska-yellow-cedar because its wood turns sulfur-yellow when wet.

Hemlocks (*Tsuga*)

Hemlocks are noted for short needles and droopy tops and branches. There are only about 10 species of hemlock in the world, mostly in North America, China, and Japan. Oregon has two hemlocks: the abundant and commercially important western hemlock and the lesser known mountain hemlock. Even when found growing together, they're easy to tell apart.

Mountain hemlock: needles are blue-green on all surfaces, are similar in size, and are uniformly arranged around the twig. Clusters of needles often have a starlike appearance. Cones are cylindrical and are 1 to 3 inches long.

Western hemlock: needles are all very short, but have distinctly different sizes on the same twig. They are yellow-green on top and have two white bands on their undersides. They tend to stick out the sides of the twigs but also are on top of the twig. Cones are egg-shaped and about 1 inch long.

mountain hemlock (*Tsuga mertensiana*)

Size: Grows to 100' tall and 3' in diameter.

Needles: Under 1" long; blue-green in color; star-like appearance on short shoots.

Fruit: Woody cones 1–3" long; thin, rounded scales.

Twigs: Moderately stout; many short shoots; terminal branch tips have a natural bend.

Bark: Reddish-brown with narrow ridges; about 1" thick.

Elevation is the key. Mountain hemlock is always found near treeline, braving the fury of mountain storms. Generally, it grows above the range of western hemlock, but not always. Oregon has a considerable amount of mountain hemlock, always in high, remote locations. Outside of Oregon, mountain hemlock ranges from southeast Alaska to central California and eastward into the northern Rockies.

Star-spangled tree. Perhaps the most distinctive feature of mountain hemlock is clusters of needles with a starlike appearance. Although individual needles are similar to those of other conifers, many grow on short shoots and stick out from all sides, giving the appearance of thousands of stars on each branch. Its short needles (under 1 inch long) tend to have a blue-green color that makes them highly prized as ornamentals. Cones are generally 1 to 3 inches long and have thin, smooth scales. The top of the tree and all the branch tips are bent, almost appearing to be broken.

Uses. When they reach sufficient size, mountain hemlocks are harvested for pulp and lumber, but their growth rates are slow, and many groves are set aside in parks and wilderness areas for their aesthetic beauty.

western hemlock *(Tsuga heterophylla)*

Size: Grows to 200' tall and 4' in diameter.

Needles: Short (under ¾" long); several distinct sizes; green above and white underneath each needle; most needles appear to arise from the sides of the twigs.

Fruit: Small, woody cones (about 1"); egg-shaped; thin, smooth scales.

Twigs: Thin and droopy; leaf scars are partially raised pegs.

Bark: Thin (under 1"); flattened ridges; inner bark is reddish with purple streaks.

Droopy top and bobbing branches. Mother Nature put a waving banner at the very top of western hemlock, making it easy to identify, even from a fast-moving car. The leader, or highest tip, droops over like a buggy whip. Other trees that resemble hemlock—true firs, spruces, and Douglas-fir—have stiff, erect leaders. False cedars also have flexible leaders, but their flat sprays of scalelike leaves are unlike hemlock.

Unique needles. To identify western hemlock, notice the short needles that pop out on top of the twigs. The other needles are usually in ranks like soldiers, but not those short ones—they are in disarray. Western hemlock needles are thin, flat, and blunt—almost as blunt as the end of your finger. While they differ noticeably in length, they average less than ½ inch—the shortest needles of any conifer in this region. Hemlock cones are also very small—about 1 inch long—and when open, they're shaped like an egg. Individual trees often bear tremendous numbers of cones.

Changing importance. Remember the fairy tale of Cinderella, who was treated as a household drudge and later became a prince's wife? Hemlock has a Cinderella story because as late as 1930, lumbermen did not want it. They could not market it, so immense volumes were wasted during logging. But times have changed. No tree exceeds western hemlock in pulp quality and yield for high-quality newsprint and book, magazine, and tissue papers. Napoleon, the famous French general, said that an army moves on its stomach; a modern society moves on paper—in the 1980s the average American consumed over 600 pounds per year! Western hemlock is also used for plywood, and for some solid wood products. Gym floors are frequently made of hemlock because its wood resists mechanical abrasion better than other softwoods and becomes harder with age.

Hemlock ecology. Western hemlock can thrive in heavy shade. Therefore, its seedlings can fight their way through thick patches of competing vegetation and form dense, multilayered "climax forests," in which young hemlocks grow under older hemlocks and Douglas-firs. Its tolerance to shade also enables trees to grow close together. As a result, forests that include western hemlock grow more wood per acre than any other forest, except possibly the remarkable redwoods. The thin bark of western hemlock makes it vulnerable to serious insect and disease attacks, and shallow roots put it at risk to windthrow. Hemlocks shower incredible numbers of far-flying seeds, so tiny that 1 pound may contain 300,000 of them! Foresters have noted hemlock seedlings growing as thick as grass—as many as 5 million to the acre. The seeds sprout easily and can even be found on rotting stumps and mossy logs (often called "nurse logs" because they nurture so many seedlings).

Loves cool, cloudy conditions. The more rain and fog, the more western hemlock seems at home. It loves deep shade and the crowding of neighboring trees. This tree with its graceful feathery limbs is a good rainfall indicator. At 60 inches of rain per year, it masses in dense, dark forests of the Coast and Cascade ranges; below 60 inches, it becomes scarce. Western hemlock stretches from southeastern Alaska to northern California and eastward into the northern Rockies. It's the state tree of Washington.

Finest book and magazine papers

The tolerant tree wins. How?

Junipers (*Juniperus*)

Junipers are strange conifers indeed. Their fruits look like blue berries, and their leaves may be either scalelike or needlelike. In fact, their fruits are round cones, but they're softer than most and they have a blue, red, or copper color. Junipers bear male and female flowers on separate trees, so only "female" trees have fruit. Juniper foliage may be scalelike, needlelike, or both, and it often has a distinctive odor that can be smelled from quite a distance.

Three junipers are native to Oregon, but chances are good that western juniper is the only one you will see. The two others are Rocky Mountain juniper, found sparingly in the Wallowa Valley, and common juniper, which grows primarily near treeline. Oregon's junipers do not typically grow together.

Western juniper: has both scalelike and needlelike leaves, each with a sticky, aromatic dot of resin on it; has an upright growth form; grows on hot, dry, low elevation sites in eastern Oregon. Needlelike leaves are very short and commonly are called "awl-like."

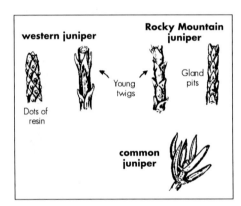

Common juniper: grows primarily at high elevations; has a shrublike or matted growth form; has individual needlelike leaves about ½ inch long. (Grows only as a shrub in Oregon, so will not be described further)

Rocky Mountain juniper: resembles western juniper, except that its needles do not have resin dots. Grows along the Idaho border. (So rare in Oregon that it will not be described further.)

western juniper (*Juniperus occidentalis*)

Size: Grows to 60' tall and 3' in diameter, but most often smaller. Commonly has short, multiple-branched trunk.

Needles: Combination of scalelike and awl-like needles; back of each needle has a white or clear resin dot. Distinctive fragrance.

Fruit: Small, round, blue "berry" (actually a nonwoody cone).

Bark: Thin, reddish-brown, and fibrous.

Distinctive tree. Western juniper is known by everyone who lives in eastern Oregon. Western junipers are small evergreen trees with thin shreddy bark, bluish "berries," and tiny, scalelike needles that are scratchy to the touch. Each scale has a small gland on its back where there is, or was, a tiny bead of resin that seals the breathing pore to conserve moisture. Juniper "berries" are really cones with soft scales that seldom open. They take 2 years to mature and have a bluish-white coating (called bloom) that can be rubbed off. The resin inside these berries has a strong distinctive odor of its own. In Oregon, "home on the range" means the scent of western juniper and sagebrush.

One sprig fills room like burning incense

The camel of trees. As you emerge from mountainous forests into eastern Oregon's "treeless" regions, you enter an extensive, open juniper woodland. Western juniper grows throughout the arid West but seems to find a special home in central Oregon. Western juniper is the "camel" of our trees, living on less water in dry climates than any other Oregon tree. Where it has moisture, western juniper will grow more than 50 feet tall, but typically it's smaller. Although it usually grows alone, it may be joined by ponderosa pine if rainfall is above 12 inches.

Makes the prairie hills look like polka-dot

More about juniper. Despite their short stature, western junipers commonly live to be several hundred years old. In the great juniper groves of central Oregon, some grow to be 4 to 5 feet thick. Half-dead, gnarled, and ghostlike, they tell of a tenacious struggle to survive where no other tree can. Ogden Wayside near Terrebonne has a sample of these ancient and craggy junipers, a different but memorable forest. The scientific name, *occidentalis*, means western, referring to the fact that it grows in western North America.

Ancient, gnarled junipers in Deschutes are scenic feature

Uses. The wood of western juniper is used mainly for fuel, fence posts, and gift shop novelties. Fence posts made of durable juniper heartwood are said to outlast two post holes. Deer and cattle browse the foliage, while birds and small animals feast on the berries. Northwest Indians also ate the berries.

Larches *(Larix)*

Larches are different from most conifers because they're deciduous—they lose their needles each fall. In addition, their needles are arranged differently from those of most conifers; on current-year twigs they're borne singly, but on older twigs they arise in dense clusters from stout, woody pegs that resemble wooden barrels. Only 10 species of larch grow in the world, mostly in cold parts of the northern hemisphere. Only western larch is native to Oregon, but a similar species, subalpine larch, grows in Washington, Idaho, and Canada. Larches are commonly called tamaracks, especially by people whose roots are in eastern North America.

western larch *(Larix occidentalis)*

Size: Grows to 180' tall and 4' in diameter.

Needles: Deciduous (fall from the tree in winter); borne on woody pegs in clusters of 20–40; 1–2" long; yellow-green.

Fruit: Small, woody cones (1–2" long); papery bracts are longer than scales.

Twigs: Have conspicuous pegs where needles grow.

Bark: Mature bark is furrowed and flakes off in irregularly shaped pieces. Reddish-orange.

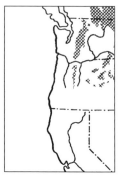

Jack Frost paints foliage

14 or more needles per bundle

Yellow in fall, naked in winter. In the fall of the year, western larch is as easy to recognize as an apple tree. Its needles turn bright yellow and drop to the ground. After standing bare all winter, larch blossoms out in new spring clothes of light green. No other western conifer is such a pale green; you can pick out a western larch as far away as colors can be seen.

Identifying western larch. Western larch is the only conifer native to Oregon that sheds its needles in winter. This alone makes it easy to identify. Other features that help identify western larch include needles that are clustered on stout, woody pegs, and "whiskery" cones. Old larches have colorful reddish bark that flakes off in jigsaw puzzle pieces (similar to ponderosa pine). The trunk of western larch is straight as a flagpole, and the crown is so open you can see the entire trunk and all its short horizontal branches. Western larch is a large, fast-growing tree for the dry forests it occupies. It's long-lived, often exceeding 500 years.

Where it grows. In Oregon, look for western larch in eastside mountain ranges between 2,000 and 7,000 feet. Although these forests are dry by westside standards, western larch likes comparatively moist locations such as north-facing slopes and valley bottoms.

Uses. Western larch produces lumber that is well liked for general construction. Higher grades have an attractive grain and are used for interior finish. It's also valuable for posts, poles, and mine timbers because of its resistance to decay. A heavy wood, larch firewood produces a great deal of heat.

Spurlike buds on winter branch, "whiskery" cones

Pines (*Pinus*)

Worldwide, pines are the most common type of conifer; there are nearly 100 different species. North America alone has more than 30. In general, pines are easy to distinguish from other needle-leaved trees because:

- Pines have long, narrow needles bound in bundles resembling whisk brooms. (Actually, some whisk brooms are made of pine needles.)

- Pines have hard, woody cones with thick, tough scales.

- Pine branches grow in distinctive "whorls" or rings that make their trunks easy to climb. (Each whorl represents 1 year's growth.)

Pine forests are also distinctive. In general, pine trees like a lot of light, so pine forests are open, and sunlight spills through to the forest floor. Wind moving through their long needles also gives pine forests a distinctive sound, and no one can miss their unique fragrance.

Eight species of pine are native to Oregon, although many others have been introduced. Four of Oregon's pines (lodgepole, sugar, ponderosa, and western white) were named by Scottish botanist David Douglas. Apparently this diversity surprised even him, for he wrote to his employer at the Royal Horticulture Society of England, "You will begin to think that I manufacture pines at my pleasure."

To identify Oregon's pines, count the needles in each bundle. This will divide the species into smaller groups. Then check the range and the appearance of the cones to pinpoint the species.

 Two needles per bundle: **lodgepole**

 Three needles per bundle: **ponderosa, Jeffrey,** and **knobcone**

 Five needles per bundle: **western white, sugar, limber,** and **whitebark**

lodgepole pine *(Pinus contorta)*

(commonly called **shore pine** along the coast)

Size: Grows to 100' tall and 2' in diameter. Typically very slender.

Needles: Two needles per bundle; 1–3" long; commonly twisted.

Fruit: Small, egg-shaped cones (1–2" long), often with a prickle. May remain closed on the tree for years.

Bark: Thin, dark, and flaky.

Two-needled pine. Lodgepole pine is easy to identify because it's the only two-needled pine native to Oregon. Also, its cones and needles are much smaller than those of our other pines. The needles are 1 to 3 inches long and twist apart from one another—leading to the scientific name "*contorta*." The prickly, egg-shaped cones are seldom longer than 2 inches, and may hang on the tree unopened for many years, waiting for the heat of fire to release their seeds.

Where lodgepole pine grows. Lodgepole pine is one of the most widely distributed trees in North America. Two varieties of lodgepole pine grow in the Northwest—a coastal form, often called "shore" pine, and a mountain form, simply called "lodgepole." Shore pines grow within a few miles of the coast and are typically bushy and distorted—their buds and branches continually blasted by sand and salt crystals driven by gale-force winds. Although they're not important commercially, they do help stabilize sand dunes, and they add to the beauty of Oregon's coast. The mountain form of lodgepole, on the other hand, occupies extensive areas at middle and high elevations throughout eastern Oregon and is an important timber tree. Its growth form is typically tall, straight, and very slender.

Meaningful name. The mountain lodgepole grows slim and straight to 80 or even 100 feet. The name seems to have

originated with Lewis and Clark. They noted that American Indians of the Great Plains traveled to the Rocky Mountains for the slender "lodgepoles" upon which to raise their lodges or teepees. Such lodgepoles would be used for a lifetime, until worn out by weathering and handling.

Small tree, large numbers. The western states hold immense supplies of lodgepole pine. Abundant reproduction causes "dog-hair" thickets where growth stagnates unless it's thinned, either by wildfire or by humans. Lodgepole's economic future appears linked to industries making paper or composition boards for which pine fiber is excellent and large trees are unnecessary. The main uses today are for lumber, poles, posts, house logs, and fiber products.

Fire-related species. With age and overcrowding, lodgepole pine becomes vulnerable to attack from a variety of insects and diseases. Epidemic pine beetle infestations in Oregon in the 1970s, 1980s, and 1990s have killed several hundred thousand acres of trees. Once dead, these dense lodgepole stands are very susceptible to wildfire. Fortunately for lodgepole, it's well prepared; its small, hard cones remain on the tree unopened until a fire passes through. When the flames die, the cones open, spreading their seeds across the charred ground. As a result, lodgepole seedlings can grow with limited competition from other species.

Size: Grows to 180' tall and 6' in diameter.

Needles: Grow in bundles of 3 (rarely 2); 5–10" long; tufted near the ends of branches.

Fruit: Egg-shaped; 3–5" long; each scale has a straight, stiff prickle.

Bark: Flakes off in shapes like jigsaw puzzle pieces. Older trees have a distinct yellow or orange color.

ponderosa pine *(Pinus ponderosa)*

Oregon's number-two tree. Ponderosa pine is the most widely distributed pine in North America. It grows from the Pacific coast to South Dakota and from Canada to Mexico. It's the state tree of Montana. In Oregon, it's almost as prominent east of the Cascades as Douglas-fir is west of that range. The scientific name of this tree, *Pinus ponderosa*, is almost the same as its common name. Lewis and Clark made note of this abundant pine in 1804, but it was David Douglas of Douglas-fir fame who named it in 1826. The name "ponderosa" refers to the ponderous or heavy wood.

Recognizing ponderosa. Its needles are 5 to 10 inches long and nearly always grow in bundles of three, but two's sometimes can be found. Groups of needles are tufted at the ends of the branches. Ponderosa's egg-shaped cones are 3 to 6 inches long and each scale is tipped with a short, straight prickle.

Unique bark. While the bark of young ponderosa pine is nearly black, the bark of mature trees is commonly pumpkin orange; in fact, large old trees are often called "punkins." Almost regardless of age, the bark of ponderosa flakes off in small, irregular pieces resembling the pieces of a jigsaw puzzle. Bark crevices of older trees and cut branches have a pleasing, "pitchy" smell, similar to turpentine. At the base of old trees, look for small flakes of bark; you'll discover the most fanciful shapes reminding you of all kinds of creatures.

Bark of old trees sheds curious, jigsaw-puzzle flakes

Where ponderosa pine grows. Ponderosa pine generally likes warm and sunny places, but can tolerate severe winters. Productive forests grow with as little as 15 inches of annual rain. Almost half the trees east of the Cascade summit in Oregon are ponderosa pines. In southwest Oregon, ponderosa pine grows down the western slope of the Cascades. Surprisingly to many, ponderosa pines also are found scattered across the Willamette Valley, where they have a good ability to tolerate wet winter soils. In fact, many ponderosa plantations are being established on sites too wet for Douglas-fir. Ponderosa pine is long-lived, frequently exceeding 500 years; one Oregon Methuselah attained 726 years. (Methuselah is a biblical person who is supposed to have attained 969 years of age.)

What ponderosa is used for. Ponderosa pine is prized for lumber and many other uses. In fact, the wood is claimed to be the most versatile of any found in North America. It's made into lumber for residential and other light construction, furniture, millwork (such as window frames, doors, stairs, and molding), boxes and crates, and specialty items such as toys, fence pickets, slats, and novelties.

Doors, sash, knotty pine walls

Unusual Oregon pines. Standing a stone's throw from the Deschutes River, 32 miles south of Bend, is a ponderosa nearly 9 feet in diameter. Eighteen miles west of Grants Pass, the Siskiyou National Forest has one that is 246 feet tall (possibly the world's tallest). Northeastern Lake County has the "Lost Forest," a 9,000-acre island of ponderosa pine some 40 miles out in the desert. This strange grove exists on 10 inches of rain annually because special ground conditions trap moisture beneath the sand.

Forests to enjoy. Ponderosa grows to a large size, and no other forest of our region can match the splendor of the older trees. Their bark fairly glows in the sunlight. There is enough color and beauty for a forest of make-believe where you might run into Hansel and Gretel or even Smokey the Bear. Naturally, movie makers choose the photogenic ponderosa forests for their forest scenes. Vacationers choose ponderosa country because this tree grows where the summer climate is most agreeable to people.

Fire in the forest. Ponderosa pine forests have evolved with fire; in fact, their health depends on it. Because ponderosa forests grow in dry, grassy environments, summer lightning fires are common. If fires occur often enough, the stands stay thinned and healthy. If fires are inhibited, stands become dense and stagnated. Individual trees become stressed and susceptible to insects and disease, such as western pine beetles and dwarf mistletoe. When a fire finally does occur in a dense stand, many of the trees are killed. When fires are not suppressed by humans, ponderosa pine forests experience small ground fires every 10 to 20 years. Most of the beautiful, yellow-bellied stands that people so admire in eastern Oregon owe their existence to frequent, light fires.

Seen in films

Jeffrey pine *(Pinus jeffreyi)*

Size: Grows to 140' tall and 4' in diameter.

Needles: Grow in bundles of 3 (rarely 2); 5–10" long; often "bushy" along twig.

Fruit: Large, woody cones; 5–12" long; each scale has a curved (J-shaped) prickle.

Bark: Flakes off in pieces like a jigsaw puzzle's. Older bark is distinctly reddish-brown.

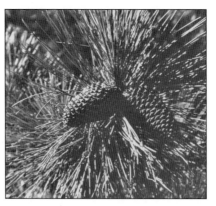

Another three-needled pine. Jeffrey pine is another Oregon pine with needles clasped in threes. In fact, Jeffrey's needles are so similar to ponderosa's that the two are difficult to tell apart. However, Jeffrey pine has a thicker and larger cone—one that resembles an old-fashioned beehive or a

pineapple. While Jeffrey's cones can vary in length from 5 to 12 inches, the typical huge oval is hard to mistake. One additional difference: the prickles on the ends of Jeffrey's cone scales are curved (or J-shaped), while ponderosa's are straight. Expert observers also seem able to single out Jeffrey pine by subtle differences such as a purplish-white bloom on its new twigs (not seen on ponderosa), a pineapplelike odor, or the bark color of old trees: reddish-brown in the case of Jeffrey and yellowish-brown to orange for ponderosa. Because Jeffrey holds its needles longer than ponderosa, Jeffrey's branches typically have a bushier look than ponderosa's.

Where it grows. Jeffrey pine has a limited range in Oregon, growing only in the southwest corner of the state. However, it grows throughout California, sharing its range with ponderosa pine. Jeffrey pine can tolerate a wide variety of soils and widely fluctuating temperatures. It's one of the few trees that can grow on serpentine soils, whose high levels of calcium and magnesium are toxic to most plants.

Uses. Jeffrey pine is used in the same ways as ponderosa pine and often is sold as ponderosa pine.

Distinguishing Ponderosa Pine from Jeffrey Pine

Cones: Cones are the best way to tell these two species apart. The cones of both species are relatively large and egg-shaped. Jeffrey cones, however, are typically much larger—5 to 12 inches long—and each cone scale ends in a prickle that curves in (often said to be J-shaped). Ponderosa cones are typically 3 to 5 inches long, and their scales end in a prickle that sticks out.

Needles: Needles are similar for the two species, typically growing in bundles of three but sometimes two. In both species, they're typically 5 to 10 inches long. One difference is that ponderosa pine holds its needles for only 2 to 3 years; therefore they appear tufted near the ends of branches. Jeffrey pine holds its needles for 5 to 8 years; therefore the branches often appear to be more bushy.

Bark: In both species, the bark flakes off in puzzle-like pieces. Some people can detect a subtle difference in color in old trees: Jeffrey pine tends to be reddish-brown, while ponderosa tends to be yellowish- or orangish-brown. Some people can smell a difference: Jeffrey's bark often smells sweet, like vanilla or pineapple, while ponderosa's bark smells "pitchy," like turpentine.

ponderosa pine   Jeffrey pine

knobcone pine *(Pinus attenuata)*

Size: A small tree, up to 80' tall and 2' in diameter. Often has multiple, crooked tops.

Needles: Grow in bundles of 3; 3–7" long; slender and twisted.

Fruit: Woody cones with swollen, knoblike bumps on one side; 3–6" long; grow in dense clusters.

Bark: Dark and scaly.

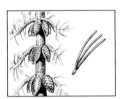

Another three-needled pine. Knobcone pine bears its 3- to 7-inch long needles in groups of three, like ponderosa and Jeffrey pines. However, knobcone's needles are thinner and more twisted than are the two others.

Distinctive cones. No one will mistake the odd cones of knobcone pine. They encircle the branches and trunk of the tree in dense, tightly clinging clusters. The side of each cone facing away from the twig is distinctly swollen and contains rock-hard, knoblike projections that give the tree its common name. These clusters may remain on the tree so long that they're overgrown by the wood—creating quite a surprise for woodcutters "bucking up" knobcone pine for firewood!

Fire-dependent tree. Knobcone pine depends on fire for its very existence. Its cones are rock hard and remain on the tree unopened until the heat from a fire causes them to crack. The seeds inside can remain viable for up to 50 years. When the seeds do flutter to the burned ground, they're likely to find the bright light and bare soil they need to flourish. Without fire, knobcone pines eventually will be replaced by tree species that are more tolerant of shade.

Uses. Knobcone pine is a small, shrubby tree that commonly has multiple tops. Because of this, it's used primarily for firewood. It also helps pave the way for new forests following wildfire.

Range. Although knobcone pine grows throughout California, it grows only in the southwestern corner of Oregon. Typically, it prefers hot, dry, low elevation sites (1,000 to 2,000 feet) that are frequented by wildfires.

western white pine *(Pinus monticola)*

Size: A large tree, growing to 180' tall and 4' in diameter.

Needles: Grow in clusters of 5; 2–4" long; white lines on 2 sides of each needle.

Fruit: Woody cones, 5–12" long; slender and curved. Cone scales are thin and often curve up on the end.

Bark: Dark; broken into squares or rectangles on older trees. Bark often "ringed" where a whorl of branches once grew.

Five-needled pine. Western white pine has five needles in each bundle. Throughout most of Oregon this alone is enough to identify it—except in the southern Cascades where sugar pine grows, and near treeline where you might find whitebark or limber pine. Sugar and western white pines are large forest trees when mature; limber and whitebark pines are small trees of open, wind-swept slopes.

Distinctive cones. The cones of western white pine are one of its most distinctive features. They range in length from 5 to 12 inches, and they commonly have a graceful curve, similar to a banana's. Their scales are thin, turned up on the end, and commonly are covered with white, sticky resin. Western white pine cones are a favorite for holiday wreaths and mantle decorations.

Uses. Carpenters enjoy working with western white pine because it has a light, smooth, attractive wood that planes and saws easily. It's similar to eastern white pine, the top-ranked American wood for nearly 300 years. Western white pine has many important lumber uses, much like those listed for ponderosa pine. Most wood matches are of western white pine, and it's a favorite of woodcarvers.

More about white pine. Although it grows at middle elevations throughout much of Oregon, western white pine does not grow in pure stands. Instead, it grows in mixed forests along with Douglas-fir, true firs, and several other pines. Western white pine doesn't care who knows its age: simply count the whorls of limbs on a white pine, and you will know how old it is. Douglas-fir and true firs show this habit too, but less clearly. Western white pine is the state tree of Idaho, and its scientific name, *monticola*, means "of the mountains."

Count the whorls

Tree-killing fungus. White pine blister rust is a fungus that attacks and kills all five-needled pines. Because it must spend one stage of its life on leaves of currant and gooseberry bushes, a great effort was made to eliminate these shrubs from the forest. However, this proved impracticable; wind-blown rust spores travel too far and too fast. The fungus, inadvertently imported from France in the early 1900s, continues to kill and injure many trees. However, rust-resistant strains do occur in nature, and foresters are taking advantage of this genetic resistance to improve white pine's chances of survival.

sugar pine *(Pinus lambertiana)*

Size: Grows to over 200' tall and 7' in diameter. The tallest of all the pines.

Needles: Five needles per cluster; 2–4" long; bloom (white coloring) on all 3 surfaces of each needle.

Fruit: Huge, woody cones (10–20" long) with thin scales.

Bark: Reddish-brown and furrowed (no blocky patches, and no rings where whorls of branches once grew).

Resembles white pine, so learn both

Look for big cones. Like western white pine, sugar pine has needles in bundles of five. However, sugar pine's huge cones make it easy to identify. They average over 1 foot long and dangle from the tips of long upper limbs, bending them downward like a stubborn fish pulling on a fishing pole. Green cones can weigh 3 or 4 pounds, and it's "bombs away!" when squirrels drop them from 100 feet up—campers beware! Although sugar pine is common throughout the forests of southwest Oregon, it never grows in pure stands. It prefers moist, well-drained spots in the sun and grows only in the mountains of Oregon and California.

"The priests of pine." John Muir, the famous early-American naturalist, greatly admired sugar pine. Observing these large trees in the forest, he said: "They are ever tossing out their immense arms in what might seem the most extravagant gestures. . . They are the priests of pine and seem ever to be addressing the surrounding forest. . . The yellow pine is found growing with them on warm hillsides, and the white silver fir on cool northern slopes; but noble as these are, the sugar pine is easily king and spreads his arm above them in blessing while they nod and wave in signs of recognition."

What it's used for. Sugar pine belongs to a group known as soft or white pines, which have light, soft, easily worked wood of high value. Sugar pine's uses are similar to those of western white pine. Like western white pine, sugar pine is susceptible to white pine blister rust.

A narrow escape. David Douglas, the young Scottish botanist for whom Douglas-fir is named, nearly lost his life on the day he found the sugar pine (October 26, 1826). Near Oregon City he had seen large pine seeds in a Northwest Indian's pouch, and he had gone into southern Oregon in search of the tree that grew such huge seeds. Near Roseburg, Douglas found the tree. To get some of the cones, which he said hung from their branches "like small sugar loaves in a grocer's shop," he shot them down with his gun. Attracted by the noise, local Indians came and threatened him, but he drew two guns and prepared to fight, so they finally went away.

Taste treat. The cones of sugar pine are the longest of any pine in the world, although they're not as heavy as the fearsome, spiny cones of California's Coulter pine. Their seeds are also large, and very tasty. Each seed is as big as a kernel of corn and its wing is from 1 to 2 inches long. The name sugar pine comes from the sugary tasting globules of resin that drip from wounds to the trunk or branches. Northwest Indians were fond of this resin, but they were careful not to eat too much of it because of its laxative effect. Sugar pines sometimes grow more than 200 feet tall—the tallest of all the pines.

Distinguishing Western White Pine from Sugar Pine

Cones: Cones are the best way to tell these two species apart. Western white pine cones are 5 to 12 inches long, slender, and curved; their scales are thin and turn up on the ends. Sugar pine cones are typically over a foot long, and sometimes reach 20 inches. In addition, they're much fatter than western white pine cones and they're straight; their scales are typically thick and straight.

Bark: The bark of large western white pines is broken into small squares that resemble bathroom tile or the back of an alligator. Its color is dark gray to black. On large trees, sugar pine bark is broken into long plates and is reddish-brown. The bark of sugar pine begins to break up into narrow plates on trees as small as 4 inches in diameter, while the bark of white pine is noticeably smooth on young trees.

Needles: In both species, each single needle has three sides. In sugar pine, each side has several white lines. In western white pine, only two sides have white lines.

western white pine

sugar pine

limber pine *(Pinus flexilis)*

Size: Usually under 50' tall and 2' in diameter. Often shrubby.

Needles: Clusters of 5; 2–3" long; white lines on all surfaces.

Fruit: Woody cones, 3–7" long; thick scales with no prickles. Seeds have terminal wings.

Bark: Grayish-brown with furrows and ridges.

Small, five-needled pine. Limber pine is a five-needled pine, like western white, sugar pine, and whitebark pine. Limber pine is much smaller and much less common than sugar and western white pine, so those three are not likely to be confused. However, limber and whitebark pines are quite similar. Limber pine gets its name from long, slender branches that are so flexible they can be tied in knots. Limber pine typically has a short, crooked trunk with many large, spreading branches.

Comparison with whitebark pine. Limber and whitebark pines are easily confused. Where their ranges overlap, in the northern Rockies, they grow in similar habitats, have similar growth forms, and have five needles per fascicle. Both begin life with a smooth, grayish white bark, though limber pine bark darkens with age. Cones are a principal difference. Limber pine cones generally are larger than whitebark cones and turn from green to brown as they ripen. When limber pine seeds are ripe, their cone scales open and the seeds fall to the ground. Once seeds are shed, the cones commonly fall to the ground still intact. Whitebark cones usually are smaller and remain purple throughout their development. Typically, nutcrackers and jays pick them to pieces while they still are on the tree; as a result, usually only pieces of whitebark cones are found on the ground. Both trees are important food sources for birds and small mammals and even for some larger ones such as bears.

Tree of high elevations. In Oregon, limber pine grows only in the Wallowa Mountains, an offshoot of the Rockies. It's typically found on open, windy ridges near tree line. Continually blasted by snow, ice, and sand, it often has a single upright stem surrounded by a low, dense, matted tangle of branches.

whitebark pine *(Pinus albicaulis)*

Size: Usually under 50' tall and 2' in diameter. Often distorted or shrublike.

Needles: Clusters of 5; 1–3" long; faint white lines on all surfaces.

Fruit: Small, woody cones; 1½–3" long; thick scales with no prickles. Cone's scales stay closed even when seeds mature. Seeds are unwinged.

Bark: Thin, scaly, and light gray throughout its life.

Small, five-needled pine. Whitebark pine is a small, five-needled pine, similar in appearance to limber pine. However, its cones are smaller than those of limber pine, and it's much more widely distributed in Oregon and Washington than is limber pine. When mature, the cones of whitebark pine are purple, and they remain on the tree with scales closed for at least 1 year. The seeds are unwinged and resemble small pebbles, which is why whitebark is grouped with the stone pines. The bark of whitebark pine retains a grayish-white color throughout its life, giving rise to its common name. Like limber pine, its twigs are as flexible as rope.

For the birds. The lifecycle of whitebark pine is integrally linked to that of Clark's nutcrackers (and several species of jays). These long-beaked birds have the ability to reach inside the scales of mature whitebark pine cones and pluck out the ripe seeds. Many of the seeds are eaten immediately and form a vital food source for these birds, but many more are cached (stored in the ground) for later use. Some sprout there, forming the basis for a new population of pine trees. As a result, Clark's nutcrackers and whitebark pines are almost totally dependent on each other for survival. Birds with smaller, thicker beaks and sharp-toothed mammals often break the scales off to get at the seeds held tightly inside.

Found in the Cascades. Whitebark pine grows at the tree line throughout the Cascades and in the northern Rockies, clinging to the harshest sites that trees can endure. While it can tolerate terrific cold and wind, it's usually distorted and bushlike. Timberline trees no taller than an adult person have been found to be 500 years old.

Redwood *(Sequoia)*

Redwoods have an interesting taxonomic history. Although several species of redwood *(Sequoia)* once spread across the globe, long-term climate changes have reduced their numbers and their range. Now, only one species exists, *Sequoia sempervirens*, and it occupies a narrow band along the west coast of North America, from southwestern Oregon to Monterey, California.

Two other trees are commonly confused with redwoods, but each is a separate genus: giant sequoia, *Sequoiadendron*, and dawn redwood, *Metasequoia*. Before the Cascades formed, when Oregon's climate was warmer and wetter, all three "redwoods" grew here. Now, giant sequoia grows naturally only in California, while dawn redwood is native to China. As with redwood, each of these trees has been widely planted outside its native range. Giant sequoia is widely planted as an ornamental tree in Oregon and is described in the section of this book entitled "Oregon's Principal Urban Trees."

Size: Grows to 370' tall and 23' in diameter.

Needles: About 1" long; green on top with white bands below; grow in a flat plane.

Fruit: Small, woody cones about 1" long; thick, wrinkled scales.

Twigs: Green at first, but turn brown after several years. No leaf scars present. Twigs and leaves are shed intact.

Bark: Very thick (up to 12"); reddish-brown and fibrous.

redwood *(Sequoia sempervirens)*

(sometimes called **coast redwood**)

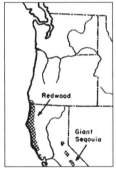

Limited range. Although redwood is commonly associated with coastal California, it also grows in southwestern Oregon. In fact, before the Cascades formed, redwoods grew throughout the Pacific Northwest. Now, Oregon's redwoods are confined to a few river valleys and mountain slopes in Curry County.

What's in a name? The common name, redwood, comes from the reddish-brown color of the heartwood. The Latin name for the genus, *Sequoia*, honors Chief Sequoyah, the Cherokee Indian who invented an alphabet for his people. The species name, *sempervirens*, means evergreen, perhaps in reference to its foliage or perhaps because of its tendency to sprout following injury. At one time, this genus included giant sequoia, but after much botanical debate, giant sequoia was placed in its own genus, *Sequoiadendron*. Now "cousins," the two species commonly are grouped together under the name California redwood and together are the state tree of California.

How to know redwood. On most twigs, the leaves are needlelike, about 1 inch long, and lie in two flat rows. Each is shaped like a double-edged sword. Needles on a twig are of unequal lengths, becoming uniformly shorter near both ends. On branches that bear cones, needles may be shaped like sewing awls—short, sharp, and rapidly tapering. Redwood cones are cylindrical, generally under 1 inch long, and are made up of thick, wrinkled scales. The bark is distinctive: reddish-brown, thick, fibrous, and deeply furrowed.

Uses of redwood. The wood is said to have "just about every characteristic that makes for the ideal." It has color, beauty, great resistance to insects and decay, and other special qualities. Further, large sizes and clear material are readily available. House siding, interior paneling, laminated structural timbers, and shakes are leading uses. Among the many specialty products are wine vats, greenhouses, fences, and outdoor furniture. Bark products include insulation, mulch, and chemicals.

Famous tree. Despite its small range, redwood is one of the world's most famous trees. Its magnificent size (trees commonly surpass 300 feet in height and 10 feet in diameter), the density of its stands (trees grow so close together that it's truly difficult to see the forest for the trees), its astonishing longevity (many surpass 1,000 years old), and its limited extent (redwoods occupy less than 0.2 percent of the commercial forest land in the United States), have combined to make redwoods the center of a worldwide conservation movement. As a result, many redwood stands are protected in national, state, and local parks.

Natural enemies. Redwood has few natural enemies. Chemicals stored in its heartwood protect it from most insects and diseases. Soft, spongy bark that commonly reaches 12 inches thick protects it from all but the most severe fires. The ability to sprout both roots and shoots from its trunk helps it recover from mud deposits that commonly occur in its flood-prone river bottom habitat. The ability to sprout also helps it regenerate following logging and fires.

¾ to 1 inch

leaves

¼ to ¾ inch

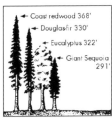

← Coast redwood 368'
← Douglas-fir 330'
← Eucalyptus 322'
← Giant Sequoia 291'

World's tallest known species (1964 survey)

REDWOOD - LET'S QUIT

Spruces (Picea)

Many people think that spruces, Douglas-firs, and the true firs look alike. In a general way they do, but look more closely. Feel the needles. If you dropped from an airplane into a Northwest forest and felt tree needles sticking you like pins, the tree would have to be a spruce. Spruces have stiff, prickly needles; Douglas-firs and true firs have soft, flexible needles. Each spruce needle springs from a tiny, woody peg; in fact, this peg is one of the best ways to identify a spruce. Spruce cones hang down from the branches like Douglas-fir cones (remember that true fir cones stand up), but spruce cones do not have Douglas-fir's pitchfork bracts. The scales of most spruce cones are papery thin, yet another difference. And spruce bark is scaly—Douglas-fir and the true firs have ridged bark.

There are approximately 40 different species of spruce in the world, but only three are native to Oregon, and only two of those are common. Location is probably the best clue to their identity:

Sitka spruce: grows only along the Pacific coast, from northern California through southeastern Alaska. Grows only near sea level. Needles are often (but not always) flat in cross-section and typically are very sharp.

Engelmann spruce: grows only in the Cascades and Rocky Mountains, from central British Columbia through New Mexico. Grows only at high elevations. Needles typically are square in cross-section and range from being very sharp to blunt.

Brewer spruce: grows only in the Siskiyou Mountains of southwestern Oregon and northern California. Needles typically are square in cross-section and are blunt on their ends.

Sitka spruce (Picea sitchensis)

Size: Commonly grows to 180' tall and 5' in diameter, although individuals may reach 16' in diameter.

Needles: 1" long; sharp; yellow-green; often flat (difficult to roll between your fingers). Some needles on a twig point sideways, others point forward.

Fruit: Woody cones; 1–4" long; hang down; very thin scales with jagged edges.

Twigs: Each needle is borne on a raised, woody peg.

Bark: Thin; gray-brown; scaly.

Knowing Sitka spruce. Fortunately, Oregon's two important spruces, Sitka and Engelmann, grow in separate parts of the state, for they're difficult to tell apart. Sitka spruce grows naturally only along the coast, and Engelmann spruce grows only in the mountains—although both are planted in other regions. If the two trees did grow together, you would have to look carefully to tell them apart. Sitka needles are really "needles"—the stiffest and sharpest of any tree in our region. In addition, Sitka needles are flat, and needles on top of the twig point forward, but those at the side point outward. Engelmann needles are not nearly as sharp, and all point slightly forward.

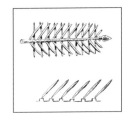

Where Sitka grows. Sitka spruce likes the cool, foggy environment of the coast. In fact, it once was called tideland spruce. In Oregon it's seldom found more than a few miles inland. In Alaska and British Columbia, it ranges farther inland. Sitka spruce is the largest spruce in the world—and the largest Sitka is a tree in Clatsop County that is more than 16 feet in diameter! Sitka spruce was named after Sitka Island (now called Baranof Island), off the coast of Alaska, and it is Alaska's state tree.

A wood with special qualities. Sitka spruce wood is very strong for its weight, which leads to many specialty uses such as ladders, aircraft shells, racing shells, garage doors, and folding bleachers. Sitka spruce is also used in pianos, organs, and violins because of its outstanding resonant qualities. The lumber is also valued for a wide range of familiar purposes. Of the paper-making woods, western hemlock and Sitka spruce are kings. Their long fibers make a strong newsprint of good color and printing qualities. Sitka spruce is among the world's fastest growing trees.

Sounding boards are spruce

Unique silhouette. When driving to the coast, it's interesting to pick out the first spruce to appear. Individuals growing in the open are unmistakable—limbs thrust out rigidly like long, pointing arms, each trailing a triangular fringe of branchlets.

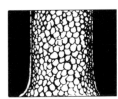

Bark like this—not in ridges

Engelmann spruce *(Picea engelmannii)*

Size: Grows to 120' tall and 3' in diameter.

Needles: 1" long; sharp; blue-green; tend to point forward; are usually square in cross-section and therefore roll between the fingers; stink when crushed.

Fruit: Woody cones about 2" long; very thin scales with jagged edges; hang down.

Twigs: Covered with distinct, raised pegs.

Bark: Thin; gray with purple tinge; scaly.

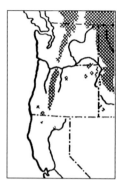

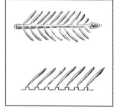

PEW! (ENGELMANN)

Similar to Sitka spruce. The cones and needles of Engelmann spruce are similar to those of Sitka spruce. However, Engelmann needles are less sharp, point uniformly toward the tip of the twig, and are definitely four-sided (Sitka needles are flatter). Because they're nearly square, Engelmann needles will roll easily between your fingers—Sitka's needles won't. In addition, Engelmann needles have an unpleasant odor when crushed. Cones of the two species are very similar.

Size and use. Engelmann spruce is a much smaller tree than its coastal cousin. Most fall short of 100 feet in height and 3 feet in diameter. The wood is used for lumber, and like other spruces it has superior paper-making properties. It's also used to make the finest violins in the world.

Range. Range is the best way to distinguish Engelmann from Sitka spruce. Engelmann ordinarily grows above 4,000 feet, often in cold, wet environments. Therefore, it's not found in the Coast Range of Oregon and Washington. Farther inland, it grows from Canada to Mexico.

Shade-tolerant tree. That means it will grow in the shade. That's why you'll find Engelmann spruces—little trees and big ones—closely mixed. Branches are held on the trunk nearly to the ground except in very dense stands.

Brewer spruce *(Picea brewerana)*

(often called **Brewer's weeping spruce**)

Size: Generally under 80' tall and 2' in diameter.

Needles: 1" long; not sharp; point toward tip of twig.

Fruit: Woody cones; 3–6" long; stiff, rounded scales with smooth edges.

Twigs: Long and drooping. Covered with distinct, woody pegs.

Bark: Thin; reddish-brown; scaly.

Known to a few explorers

Unique to southwestern Oregon. A little-known tree, Brewer spruce grows only on steep mountain slopes in the Siskiyou Mountains of southern Oregon and northern California.

Why does it weep? Does this strange tree mourn because so few people ever push into the high solitude of Josephine and Curry counties to glimpse its beauty? Stringlike branchlets 4 to 8 feet long hang down from its limbs. It's a scarce tree, but you probably would recognize it and be reminded of a weeping willow, or a very shaggy dog.

To tell it from other spruces. Its needles resemble those of Engelmann spruce, only they're even more blunt to the touch. Its cones are 3 to 6 inches long—much longer than either of Oregon's two other spruces—and its cone scales are smooth rather than jagged. Its long, weeping branches are perhaps its most distinctive characteristic.

True Firs (Abies)

True firs are so named to distinguish them from Douglas-firs, Chinese-firs, and a number of other pretenders. Sometimes they're called "balsam firs" because of tiny pockets of resin, or balsam, that are in their bark. About 40 species of true firs grow in cold regions of the northern hemisphere. True firs are well adapted to snowy environments because their short, stiff branches and pointed tops shed snow without breaking.

Seven species of true fir are native to western North America, and Oregon has six—more than any other state:

- grand fir
- noble fir
- white fir

- subalpine fir
- Pacific silver fir
- California red fir

True firs are the loveliest of conifers, adorning the scenic highlands that call to us whether young or old. Those who camp, hike, ski, hunt, or merely drive in the high country have them for fragrant companions. Scottish botanist David Douglas began the admiring names borne by so many of our true firs: noble, grand, *amabilis* (lovely) and *magnifica* (magnificent).

Recognizing True Firs

All true firs have the following characteristics:

- Cones that perch like little owls on the topmost branches—so, look aloft for large, erect cones. They often glisten with drops of fragrant, sticky resin.

- Cones of true firs do not fall intact like other conifer cones. In late fall, their scales tumble off one by one when the seeds have ripened. As a result, cones can be used to recognize true firs only in summer and early fall.

- Gently pull a needle away from its twig and notice the tiny, circular scar left on the twig. This circle makes it easy to recognize a true fir at any season.

- Young stems have fragrant resin blisters. Stick them with your finger and they pop, oozing a clear liquid. Resins and oils from the bark and foliage of true firs are used for a variety of products, including perfumes, adhesives, and pharmaceuticals. Some attribute a healing effect to this liquid.

- The buds of true firs are rounded and are often covered with resin, wax, or curved needles. Buds near the ends of twigs often grow in clusters of three or more.

Commercial Uses

True firs account for about 10 percent of the commercial timber in Oregon. They're used for lumber and plywood, and their wood fibers make superior paper. In North America, their lumber is often mixed with hemlock and sold as "Hem-Fir," but it's shipped to eastern Asia by itself where it's prized for its light color. Older true firs tend to have trunk rots caused by fungi. True firs are among our most popular Christmas trees because of their soft, fragrant foliage and their symmetrical shapes.

Telling True Firs Apart

Distinguishing between true firs is one of the most difficult tree identification tasks in Oregon. It takes patience and practice. To make things even harder, several of our species interbreed, resulting in offspring that have characteristics of both parents. Needle shape and color, twig color, cones, and location are all helpful in identifying the true firs. Start by looking to see where bloom (white or bluish-white color) is on the needles, then look for the other characteristics listed below.

If the needles have bloom on only one surface (the lower), then it's either grand fir or Pacific silver fir. Read the following two statements to decide which.

- If all the needles point to the side and grow in two distinct rows (either flat or V-shaped), then it's **grand fir**.

- If the needles do not grow in two distinct rows (if the topmost needles point forward), then it's **Pacific silver fir**.

If the needles have bloom on both sides of needles, then it's either noble fir, California red fir, subalpine fir, or white fir. Read the following statements to decide which it is.

- If the needles are shaped like hockey sticks and the young twigs are reddish-brown, it's either noble or California red fir. Read the next two statements to decide which it is.
  — If the cones are wrapped in whiskery spirals, then it's **noble fir**.
  — If the cones are not wrapped in whiskery spirals, then it's **California red fir**.

- If the needles are mostly straight and the young twigs are greenish, then it's either white fir or subalpine fir. Read the next two statements to decide which it is.
  — If most needles are less than 1 inch long and are tightly spaced on the twig, then it's **subalpine fir.**
  — If most needles are over 1½ inches long and are loosely spaced on the twig, then it's **white fir**.

grand fir *(Abies grandis)*

Size: Grows to 250' tall and 6' in diameter (but often smaller).

Needles: No bloom on upper surface. Sets of needles flattened or V-shaped.

Fruit: Upright, cylindrical cones; 3–4" long; bracts shorter than scales. Fall apart when mature.

Twigs: Terminal buds are clustered and covered with resin. Young twigs are greenish.

Bark: 2–3" thick; gray-brown and moderately furrowed; inner bark is reddish-brown.

Grand fir—the only true fir in the lowlands

Grand fir: 2-ranked and flattened

Widespread fir. Grand fir is Oregon's only true fir commonly found below 1,500 feet. Knowing this helps to identify it in western Oregon, where it once was called lowland white fir. However, it's a mountaineer too, for it ranges up to 5,000 feet. A rover, grand fir is found in all Oregon counties but one or two. Its habit is to mingle with other conifers and not to form pure stands, so its numbers are modest—perhaps 2 percent of our coniferous trees. Grand fir prefers moist locations and so is common near streams, in valleys, and on lower slopes. East of the Cascades, it's common in the mixed forest types found at middle elevations. Grand fir is very tolerant of shade, so it forms climax forests throughout much of its range.

Telling it from others. Try to identify grand fir by the foliage of its lower branches. Here, the needles will be shiny green on top (no white bloom) and will be arranged in two flattened rows, as if pressed in a book. When growing in bright light, the rows of needles may form a "V." The needles of grand fir are especially easy to confuse with Douglas-fir, but the buds and cones make it easy to tell them apart. Grand fir buds are round, and its cones are upright; Douglas-fir buds are pointed, and its cones hang down. Grand fir's cones look too much like other true fir cones to be very useful in distinguishing grand fir from other firs. In eastern and southwestern Oregon, it's often difficult to tell grand fir from white fir, for they interbreed and their offspring have characteristics of both species.

Uses. Grand fir's maximum life span of 250 to 300 years is rather short for a western conifer. Yet it's rapid growing in its youth and may attain reasonably large sizes. On some Cascade and Blue Mountain sites, its fast growth rate makes it a preferred timber species. Grand fir wood is used in the same way as the other true firs. It's also an important Christmas tree because of its lovely form, its appealing fragrance, and its rich green color.

Disease problems. Unlike Douglas-fir and most pines, the wood of true firs is not resinous—it does not exude pitch to seal off wounds—so decay-causing fungi find easy entrance. Grand fir, particularly, is subject to trunk rots. The "Indian paint" fungus often seen on grand fir east of the Cascades catches the eye. Its black conks (growths on the trunk) have brick-red insides and were used by Northwest Indians for pigments.

Pacific silver fir *(Abies amabilis)*

Size: Grows to 180' tall and 4' in diameter.

Needles: Green on top and white underneath. Top needles point forward like ski jumpers.

Fruit: Large woody cones (3–6" long); cylindrical; purple. Fall apart at maturity.

Twigs: Greenish. Buds clustered at tip are purple and covered with pitch.

Bark: Remains gray throughout its life. Resin blisters when young; scaly when older.

Useful name. The name of this species comes from the silvery white undersides of its needles. Often they seem to gleam as brightly as bicycle reflectors. The bark of trees less than 3 feet in diameter is also silvery. In some localities, foresters consider the bark alone a reliable means of identification. On older, larger trees, the bark becomes gray and scaly.

Recognizing silver fir. Unlike most true firs (except grand), Pacific silver fir's needles are green on top (no white bloom). To distinguish Pacific silver fir from grand fir, look at the needles on top of each twig. In Pacific silver fir, they lean forward like ski jumpers; in grand fir, they lie to the sides, as if neatly combed.

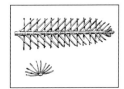

High elevation tree. Like noble fir, this species is common at middle and high elevations of the Cascades from Crater Lake north, and it appears sparsely in the higher Coast Range from Lincoln County north. However, it grows farther north into British Columbia than does noble fir. Pacific silver fir and noble fir often are found together in the northern parts of Oregon's Cascades.

Size: Grows to 200' tall and 5' in diameter.

Needles: White on both surfaces; shaped like a hockey stick. Massed on the upper surface of the twig. A tiny groove runs the length of the upper side.

Fruit: Large woody cone (4–6" long); cylindrical; has distinctive bracts that look like elephant heads. Cone falls apart at maturity.

Twigs: Reddish-brown. Buds clustered at the terminal end are over-lapped by curved needles.

Bark: Blistered on young trees. Purplish-gray to reddish-brown on mature trees; flattened ridges.

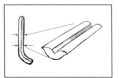

Needles from underside of twig resemble hockey sticks

That special noble look

noble fir *(Abies procera)*

Unique cones. If cones are present, noble fir is the easiest true fir to identify. As with all true firs, noble fir cones sit upright on their branches, are barrel-shaped, have thin scales with rounded "shoulders," and fall apart in the late fall after the seeds have ripened. One feature sets noble fir cones apart from the others: they're wrapped in "whiskery spirals." These whiskers are actually paper-thin bracts that separate the seeds from the cone scales. All conifers have them, but noble fir is one of the few species where they're large enough to stick outside the cone.

Needles and twigs. Needles and twigs also help identify noble fir. Needles are white on both surfaces and curve at the base like a hockey stick. Unlike other true firs (except California red fir in southern Oregon), each needle runs parallel to the twig for about ⅛ inch before it curves away. To distin-guish noble fir from California red fir, look for a tiny groove that runs the length of the upper surface of the needle—that's noble. Young noble fir twigs have a distinct reddish-brown color, and the up-curved, densely massed needles are different from other true firs. When growing in the sun, needles are tightly packed on the upper half of the twig, al-most as if they'd been neatly combed. When growing in the shade, the needles may flatten out, or take on the look of a Mohawk haircut. The foliage of noble fir is so handsome that one heavy branch with a red ribbon attached makes a perfect Christmas door swag.

Where it grows. Noble fir is truly a tree of the Pacific Northwest. It's common at middle to upper elevations the full length of the Cascades and at higher elevations in the Siskiyous. It appears sparingly in the Coast Mountains from Marys Peak north.

Uses. A fine timber species, noble fir has very strong wood for its weight. It's also one of our most popular Christmas trees and gets some use as an ornamental because of its blue color, its symmetrical growth pattern, and its unique cones.

An apt name. David Douglas found and named noble fir in 1825, paying tribute to its magnificent and noble form.

California red fir *(Abies magnifica)*

Size: Grows to 200' tall and 5' in diameter.

Needles: White on both surfaces; shaped like a hockey stick. Massed on the upper surface of the twig. A tiny ridge runs the length of the upper side.

Fruit: Large, woody cone (6–9" long); cylindrical; bracts are shorter than scales (therefore not visible). Fall apart at maturity.

Twigs: Reddish-brown. Buds clustered at the terminal end are generally not covered with resin.

Bark: Blistered on young trees. Reddish brown and deeply furrowed on mature trees.

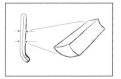

Looks like noble fir. California red fir and noble fir are nearly identical. Both are called red firs because of their reddish-brown twigs. Both have needles that have bloom on both their upper and lower surfaces, are shaped like hockey sticks, and tend to cluster on the upper sides of the twigs. One difference is that California red fir needles have a tiny ridge rising along the length of their upper surface, while noble firs have a tiny groove. Cones are the best way to tell them apart because California red fir cones do not have "whiskers" as noble fir cones do.

Rare in Oregon. California red fir is essentially a California species. In Oregon it grows only in the southern third of the Cascades and at the highest elevations in the Siskiyous. It typically grows above 4,500 feet, thriving in areas of heavy snow and long winters. North of Crater Lake, most red firs are noble firs; south of Mt. Shasta, most are California red firs. In between they may be either—or worse yet, a combination—because they hybridize where their ranges overlap.

Majestic tree. Splendid groves of large, old, California red firs enhance Sierra playgrounds such as Yosemite. The rich red-brown bark of these oldsters draws an appreciative eye. John Muir considered this tree "the most charmingly symmetrical of all the giants of the Sierra woods." The species name, *magnifica*, captures the grandeur of this tree. California red fir and its close relative, Shasta red fir, are prized as Christmas trees because of their symmetrical shape and bluish foliage.

Shasta red fir. Hybrids between noble fir and California red fir are commonly called Shasta red fir because they're so common near Mt. Shasta in northern California. These trees typically have intermediate characteristics: cones that are only partially "shingled" by protruding papery bracts, and needles that are both grooved and ridged. The scientific name of the hybrid is *Abies magnifica* variety *shastensis*.

subalpine fir *(Abies lasiocarpa)*

Size: Generally less than 100' tall and 2' in diameter.

Needles: White lines both above and below the needle; massed on the upper surface of the twig; very neat in appearance.

Fruit: Cylindrical, woody cones about 2–4" long; purple. Fall apart at maturity.

Twigs: Terminal buds are small, round, and covered with resin.

Bark: Gray; smooth or ridged. Contains resin pockets in inner bark.

Comes to fragile point like Eiffel Tower

Spirelike crown. Subalpine fir has the most arresting shape of any tree in the West. You wonder how any tree can have such a fragile, spirelike crown in such a harsh environment. Branches near the top become very short and stiff, both to shed snow and to cut wind resistance. It reminds some of the Eiffel tower and others of a church spire.

Grows at treeline. Subalpine fir knows how to "hit the high spots," rarely being found below 3,000 feet in our state. It grows abundantly in the Cascades and in the Blue Mountains, sparingly in the Siskiyous, and not at all in our Coast ranges. Near timberline, subalpine fir becomes dwarfed and contorted. On windy ridges it often forms "skirts" where the lower branches are protected under the snow from the shearing force of wind-blown ice and sand. These skirts often provide homes for young trees and protection from the elements for birds and small mammals.

Location is the best clue. In Oregon, subalpine fir can be found growing with almost any of the other true firs, especially near Crater Lake—and it's not always easy to tell them apart just by their foliage. Subalpine fir needles are white on both surfaces, are massed on the upper side of the twig, and often are very uniform, almost as it they had been manicured. Cones are bright purple and often contain large, crystal-clear resin drops where insects have bored into them. Subalpine fir is the only one of the true firs having tiny pockets of clear resin well within the thick bark. Owing to the rigors of its high homeland, subalpine fir usually is less than 100 feet tall.

Uses in nature. Thickets formed by its dense, stiff lower foliage are refuges for deer, mountain goats, and other wildlife. Squirrels feast on seeds from the large purple cones. An insect from Europe, the balsam woolly aphid, defoliates and kills subalpine, silver, and grand firs. The insect puts a sucking tube into the bark to obtain food and at the same time injects a toxin that kills trees under heavy attack. Control options are limited, but scientists have recently found several insect enemies of the aphid to help reduce its numbers.

white fir *(Abies concolor)*

Size: Grows to 200' tall and 5' in diameter.

Needles: White bloom on upper and lower surfaces; may be in distinct lines, uniformly distributed over the entire surface, or just on tips of needles.

Fruit: Upright, cylindrical cone; 3–5" long; bracts shorter than scales. Cone falls apart when mature.

Twigs: Terminal buds are clustered and slightly pitchy. Young twigs are greenish.

Bark: Grayish; thick; furrowed. Inner bark has two distinct bands of color: reddish-brown and cream (like Douglas-fir).

Confusing fir. Deep within its native range, white fir is easily distinguished from other true firs. However, in Oregon, where it crosses with grand fir, it's often difficult to distinguish from grand fir. In its pure form, white fir has long (2- to 3-inch) needles that are uniformly white on both the upper and lower surface. They turn up around the twig, resulting in a U-shaped appearance. In Oregon, the needles are commonly shorter, have distinct (and often very short) white bands on the upper needle surface, and may be flat, V- or U-shaped around the twig. As a result, white fir and grand fir often are difficult to tell apart, especially when one parent comes from each species!

Where it grows. Oregon is the northernmost frontier for white fir, which is more at home in California and the

southern Rockies. It's fairly common in southwest Oregon, especially around Crater and Klamath lakes. Stragglers reach probably the Three Sisters area in the Cascades and scattered points in the Blue Mountains.

Uses. While still alive, white fir is attacked by a variety of insects and diseases. In addition, its wood rots easily and is susceptible to frost cracking. Despite these problems, all of which result in losses at the mill, the wood is suitable for sawn products and plywood and especially for making paper. White fir's whitish hue, dense foliage, and perfect pyramidal growth form make it a prized ornamental tree. Many nurseries market it under the name "concolor fir" in recognition of its scientific name. It's also highly prized for Christmas trees in many parts of the country.

Pulp mills would like me

Identifying True Firs Can Be a Trying Experience

Identifying true firs is often difficult, especially if all six species are a possibility. Fortunately, the task can be made simpler by breaking them into groups of two. For example, only grand and Pacific silver fir do not have white bloom on the upper surface of their needles; the four other species have bloom on both their upper and lower surfaces. Only noble and California red fir have needles that are shaped like hockey sticks; the needles of other species may be gently curved, but they don't have distinct "elbows." That leaves subalpine and white fir—they have bloom on the upper surface of their needles, like noble and California red fir, but their needles do not have a distinct bend at their base that makes them look like hockey sticks. A few more clues are listed below.

Distinguishing Grand Fir from Pacific Silver Fir

These are the only two Northwest true firs whose needles are entirely green on their top surface (no white bloom). However, grand fir needles are a shiny yellow-green, and silver fir needles are a dark, rich green. Both needles have two whitish bands on their undersides, although silver fir's bands have a silvery-blue cast while grand fir's have a greenish cast. Grand fir needles are always two-ranked (although they may be flat or V-shaped); silver fir needles are not (several rows of short needles run along the top of each twig).

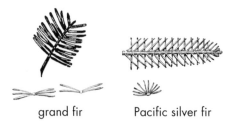

grand fir   Pacific silver fir

Distinguishing Noble Fir from California Red Fir

Both species have bluish-white bloom on both their upper and lower leaf surfaces (as do subalpine fir and white fir); both have reddish-brown twigs; and both have needles that resemble hockey sticks. How, then, can we separate them? Cones are the best clue—both grow large and upright, but noble fir cones have distinctive, papery bracts that stick out between each scale, and California red fir cones do not. Also look carefully at the top surface of each needle—noble fir has a tiny groove running down the middle, but California red fir has a ridge. Remember that hybrids have mixed characteristics.

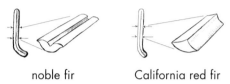

noble fir   California red fir

Distinguishing Subalpine Fir from White Fir

Although both species have greenish twigs and whitish bloom on both surfaces of their needles, there the similarity ends. Subalpine is a small tree of the subalpine region, and white fir is a large tree of middle elevations. Subalpine's needles are short, densely packed, and tightly clustered on the top side of the twig. White fir's needles are much longer, widely-spaced, and typically two-ranked (although they may be flat, V-shaped, or U-shaped).

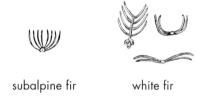

subalpine fir   white fir

Yews (Taxus)

Yew is a small genus of about eight species scattered across North America, Europe, and Asia. Although it's grouped with the conifers because it has needlelike foliage, its fruit is not a cone. Instead, it's an aril—a large, single seed surrounded by a soft, fleshy, bright red pulp. Although they look inviting, DON'T TASTE THEM, for they are highly poisonous. All yews contain a natural chemical called taxol, which is very promising in the treatment of certain types of cancer. Only one yew, Pacific yew, is native to Oregon. However, English yew is commonly planted in lawns and gardens for ornamental purposes.

Pacific yew (Taxus brevifolia)

Size: Small, understory tree. Generally under 50' tall and 2' in diameter.

Needles: About 1" long; dark green above and lighter green below (not white); pointed, but not sharp; leaf margins rolled under; needles are in a single plane.

Fruit: Small red "berry" with a single large seed (actually an aril). POISONOUS!

Twigs: Thin; remain bright green for several years. Few side branches.

Bark: Thin; purple; scaly.

Understory tree

Understory tree. Pacific yew is an inconspicuous tree most commonly found in the dark shadows of towering Douglas-firs and western hemlocks. Typically, it's small—usually under 40 feet tall—and lacks a distinctive form, sending branches wherever there's enough light to support growth. It grows very slowly, taking hundreds of years to reach its full size. If growing conditions are ideal and the forest is undisturbed for a very long time, Pacific yews may reach 75 feet tall and several feet in diameter. Pacific yew is one of the few conifers that can sprout from its base if its top is killed or damaged.

Recognizing Pacific yew. Pacific yew needles have four distinct characteristics that help separate them from other northwest conifers.

- They are two-ranked (they grow in a single plane)
- Their leaf tips come to a distinct, but soft, point
- Both sides of their needles are green (dark green above and lighter green below)
- Their edges curl under

Western hemlock and grand fir are often two-ranked but have blunt tips. Redwood is two-ranked and sharp-tipped but has two white bands on the undersides of its leaves, and its edges are not curled. Of all the conifers, Pacific yew needles are the darkest green. Pacific yew's purple, scaly bark is another good clue to its identity.

Unique fruit. Yews are the only conifers in the plant kingdom that have bright red "berries" for their fruit. The technical name for this fruit is an aril. Birds love to eat arils, but they're highly poisonous to humans, especially to small children. Yew trees are either male or female; only female trees bear the bright red arils.

Cancer-fighting bark. The bark of Pacific yew is gray and scaly on the outside but bright purple on the inside. Recently it has been found to contain a chemical called taxol. The tree manufactures taxol to protect itself from insects and disease, but scientists have found that it can help humans fight cancer.

Where it grows. Pacific yew grows from Alaska through California and in the northern Rockies. It likes shady dells, stream banks, and moist flats at medium and low elevations. Although it's widespread, it's not particularly common. It grows in small groves and as scattered individuals, not in dense stands.

How yew is used. Heavy, tough yew wood is superb for uses requiring resilience such as bows and canoe paddles. Yews of other lands once furnished bows for ancient armies. The wood has a pretty rose-red color, but the small supply limits commercial use. It's very durable in contact with the soil and so often is used for fence posts.

Archery equipment

Oregon's Native Broadleaved Trees

Although broadleaved trees from all over the world can grow in Oregon, only about 35 species are native here—and about a dozen of these commonly grow as shrubs rather than as trees. Based on the structure of their flowers and fruit, these 35 species can be grouped into about 17 genera. So, although not as economically important as the conifers, the broadleaves are a more diverse group than Oregon's conifers.

Broadleaved trees play fairly specialized roles in the forests of Oregon. In some cases, they're early successional species, occupying areas where ground has recently been disturbed by avalanches, floods, or windthrow. In other cases, they're especially adapted to hot, dry conditions, particularly where soils are shallow and moisture-holding capacities are low. In still other cases, they're able to tolerate wet soils during the growing season, an especially valuable adaptation in the large valleys of western Oregon. So, despite the fact that no single broadleaved tree dominates any of Oregon's forests, it should be clear that broadleaved trees are a vital part of Oregon's forests.

To learn to identify Oregon's broadleaved trees, turn to the broadleaf key that begins on the next page. Although it may appear complex, it's easy to use if you make one decision at a time. To learn more about Oregon's forests, turn to the section of this book called "Oregon's Forests."

To Use This Key

1. Start at the top of the key. Then read each of the two statements listed directly below the starting point.

2. Decide which of the two statements better describes the plant you're trying to identify. Then read the two statements directly under that box.

3. Continue this process until you've identified a single group of trees (called a genus). Then turn to the page indicated and read the descriptions of individual species contained within that genus (there may be only one, or there may be several).

4. If the species description matches the plant you're trying to identify—GREAT! If it doesn't match, go back to the beginning of the key and try again.

Remember, identifying trees is a bit like detective work—sometimes you need to follow false leads to discover the truth eventually.

Common Broadleaved Trees of Oregon

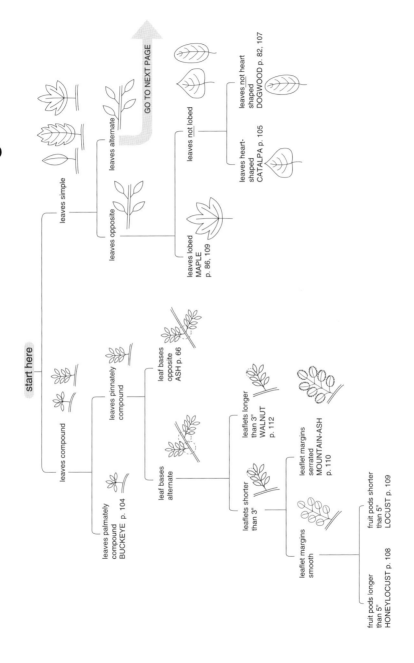

start here

leaves compound

leaves palmately compound
BUCKEYE p. 104

leaves pinnately compound

leaf bases opposite
ASH p. 66

leaf bases alternate

leaflets longer than 3"
WALNUT p. 112

leaflets shorter than 3"

leaflet margins serrated
MOUNTAIN-ASH p. 110

leaflet margins smooth

fruit pods longer than 5"
HONEYLOCUST p. 108

fruit pods shorter than 5"
LOCUST p. 109

leaves simple

leaves opposite

leaves lobed
MAPLE p. 86, 109

leaves not lobed

leaves heart-shaped
CATALPA p. 105

leaves not heart shaped
DOGWOOD p. 82, 107

leaves alternate

GO TO NEXT PAGE

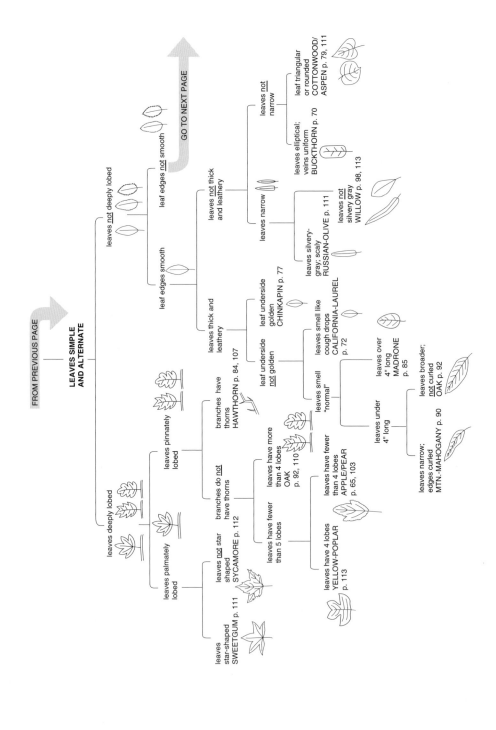

FROM PREVIOUS PAGE

LEAVES SIMPLE AND ALTERNATE

leaves deeply lobed

leaves palmately lobed

leaves star-shaped
SWEETGUM p. 111

leaves not star-shaped
SYCAMORE p. 112

leaves pinnately lobed

branches do not have thorns

branches have thorns
HAWTHORN p. 84, 107

leaves have more than 4 lobes
OAK p. 92, 110

leaves have fewer than 5 lobes

leaves have fewer than 4 lobes
APPLE/PEAR p. 65, 103

leaves have 4 lobes
YELLOW-POPLAR p. 113

leaves not deeply lobed

leaf edges smooth

leaves thick and leathery

leaf underside golden
CHINKAPIN p. 77

leaf underside not golden

leaves smell like cough drops
CALIFORNIA-LAUREL p. 72

leaves smell "normal"

leaves over 4" long
MADRONE p. 85

leaves under 4" long

leaves broader; not curled
OAK p. 92

leaves narrow; edges curled
MTN.-MAHOGANY p. 90

leaves not thick and leathery

leaves narrow

leaves silvery-gray; scaly
RUSSIAN-OLIVE p. 111

leaves not silvery gray
WILLOW p. 98, 113

leaves elliptical; veins uniform
BUCKTHORN p. 70

leaves not narrow

leaf triangular or rounded
COTTONWOOD/ASPEN p. 79, 111

leaf edges not smooth

GO TO NEXT PAGE

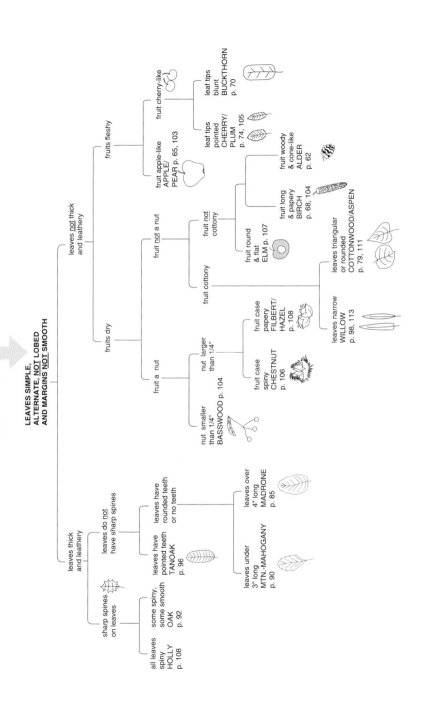

FROM PREVIOUS PAGE

LEAVES SIMPLE, ALTERNATE, NOT LOBED AND MARGINS NOT SMOOTH

leaves thick and leathery

leaves not thick and leathery

sharp spines on leaves

leaves do not have sharp spines

all leaves spiny
HOLLY
p. 108

some spiny, some smooth
OAK
p. 92

leaves have pointed teeth
TANOAK
p. 96

leaves have rounded teeth or no teeth

leaves under 3" long
MTN.-MAHOGANY
p. 90

leaves over 4" long
MADRONE
p. 85

fruits dry

fruits fleshy

fruit a nut

fruit not a nut

fruit cherry-like

fruit apple-like
APPLE/PEAR p. 65, 103

leaf tips blunt
BUCKTHORN
p. 70

leaf tips pointed
CHERRY/PLUM
p. 74, 105

nut smaller than 1/4"
BASSWOOD p. 104

nut larger than 1/4"

fruit cottony

fruit not cottony

fruit case spiny
CHESTNUT
p. 106

fruit case papery
FILBERT/HAZEL
p. 108

fruit round & flat
ELM p. 107

fruit long & papery
BIRCH
p. 68, 104

fruit woody & cone-like
ALDER
p. 62

leaves narrow
WILLOW
p. 98, 113

leaves triangular or rounded
COTTONWOOD/ASPEN
p. 79, 111

Alders *(Alnus)*

Alders like moist surroundings, and there are few creeks in western Oregon not overhung by them. Their peculiar woody cones (called strobiles) identify alders as surely as flat tails identify beavers. These strobiles hang from the trees throughout winter, like miniature lanterns. Alders shed their leaves while still green, and, therefore, return many nutrients directly to the soil. Also, alder roots contain bacteria-filled nodules that capture nitrogen from the air for the tree's use; when these roots die, the nitrogen is returned to the soil, greatly enhancing soil productivity.

Eight species of alder are native to North America. Oregon has four: red, white, Sitka, and thinleaf. Only the first two species commonly reach tree size, and only red alder is abundant. Knowing their ranges and leaf traits helps in separating one species from another.

Large Trees (40 to 80 feet tall; single trunk)

Red alder: look for leaf margins that are tightly rolled under.

White alder: leaf margins are not rolled under.

Shrubs or Small Trees (usually under 25 feet tall; commonly with multiple trunks)

Sitka alder: leaf margins have a single row of very fine teeth; margins are not rolled under (will not be described further).

Thinleaf alder: leaf margins have a double set of coarse teeth; margins are not rolled under (will not be described further).

red alder *(Alnus rubra)*

Size: Grows to 120' tall and 3' in diameter.

Leaves: Simple, alternate, and deciduous. Egg-shaped; 3–6" long. Margins doubly serrated and tightly rolled under. Veins very straight.

Fruit: Small, brown, woody "cones" about 1" long.

Twigs: Young twigs are triangular in cross-section. Buds are borne on short stalks.

Bark: Smooth, gray, and blotchy. Inner bark turns red when exposed to air.

Most common broadleaf. Red alder is the most common broadleaved tree in western Oregon and is our most important hardwood by almost any standard. It likes cool, moist environments and is everpresent in coastal forests, where it grows in dense, dark stands. Red alder is an aggressive seeder, a fast grower, and reaches "old age" at about 100 years, depending on location. Yet it may reach 120 feet in height and several feet in diameter on good sites. It's a lowland species that seldom is found above 2,500 feet. It's rare east of the Cascades and on the floor of the Willamette Valley (most valley alders are white alders).

Water loving

Unique leaves. To identify red alder, look at its leaves and bark. The leaves are large and egg-shaped. Their edges are coarsely and bluntly double-toothed (each large tooth has many smaller teeth on it). In addition, the edges are tightly rolled under (revolute), creating a distinct, green rim on the underside of each leaf. The trunk of red alder is covered with gray-white bark with black patches. It looks like a white post that a child with muddy hands and feet tried to climb. Tiny, scalelike lichens growing on the bark add to its whiteness. Young trees have greenish bark because the lichens are not yet growing on it.

Where red alder gets its name. The sapwood of red alder takes on a reddish stain when freshly cut. Northwest Indian children used to play sick by chewing the inner bark because the juice makes saliva as red as blood. *Rubra*, the scientific name for this species, is Latin for red.

Bright future. Although red alder is not a particularly large tree, it's a potentially important economic resource because of its fast growth and the large area of land it occupies. Large, straight logs are valued for cabinets, furniture, and pallet lumber. Small and crooked logs are used for toys, novelties, firewood, and pulp to make paper and composition boards. Red alder also is commonly planted in Douglas-fir forests to help sites recover from root rots and to help fertilize the site (because bacteria in their roots capture nitrogen from the air and make it usable by plants). A great deal of research is underway to find more uses for this underutilized species.

white alder *(Alnus rhombifolia)*

Size: Grows to 80' tall and 2' in diameter.

Leaves: Simple, alternate, and deciduous. Egg-shaped; 2–4" long. Margins serrated or doubly serrated; not rolled under. Veins straight.

Fruit: Small, brown, woody "cones" about 1" long.

Twigs: Have stalked buds.

Bark: Gray and splotchy; breaks into scaly ridges.

White alder leaves

Where it grows. White alder is found on both sides of the Cascades, especially along streams. It's the alder most commonly found on the floor of the Willamette Valley, but it frequently mixes with red alder in the Umpqua and Rogue valleys. White alder grows from British Columbia through much of California and eastward into Idaho and Montana.

To tell it from red alder. White alder looks very much like red alder, but three differences help separate them. First, white alder leaves typically have a single row of teeth along their edges; red alder leaves have a double row. However, some white alder leaves have wavy edges and may appear to be doubly serrate, so look carefully. Second, white alder leaves do not have revolute margins—that is, their upper surface is not rolled under. Third, white alder's bark near the ground is platy and scaly, while red alder's bark is smooth.

Uses. White alder grows too sparsely in Oregon to be commercially important, but it does capture nitrogen, recycle nutrients, and drop leafy food into streams.

Apples and Pears *(Pyrus)*

Apples and pears commonly are grouped into the same genus because their fruits are so similar. While both are easy to recognize from their flowers and fruits, they're more difficult to recognize from just their leaves. In addition, wild apples and pears commonly have different leaves from their relatives in orchards and yards. Although apples are grown throughout Oregon for both ornamental and commercial purposes, only one species is native to Oregon: western crab apple. The rest have been introduced. No pears are native to Oregon, although they're an important fruit tree.

Oregon crab apple *(Pyrus fusca)*

(sometimes listed as *Malus fusca*)

Size: Small trees that grow to 40', or large shrubs, often growing in thickets.

Leaves: Simple, alternate, deciduous. Egg-shaped; 1–4" long; margins serrated or lobed and serrated.

Fruit: Small apples (¼–¾" in diameter); yellow to red.

Twigs: Reddish-brown; spur shoots on older branches; no thorns (although some branch tips may be sharp).

Wild apples. Cultivated apples have been developed from small, bushy trees known as wild apples or crab apples because of their tart taste. Western crab apple is the only apple native to the Pacific Coast. In Oregon, it grows only west of the Cascade summit. It's especially common in coastal thickets, and it likes fence rows and the forest edge, where birds drop its seeds.

Similar to hawthorn. Oregon crab apple would be a snap to identify except for black hawthorn. They look alike, but black hawthorn has distinctive thorns and western crab apple does not (though some branch tips are nearly as sharp). Crab apple leaves may be either unlobed and serrated, or lobed and serrated—but the lobes are more sharply pointed than in hawthorn, and usually there are only three (hawthorn has many). Western crab apple has ¾-inch-long pinkish fruits that are edible but taste sharp. The flowers look like typical apple blossoms—small, white flowers in clusters.

Ashes *(Fraxinus)*

Ashes are easy to identify because they're one of the few groups of trees whose leaves are both opposite and pinnately compound. If that is not enough, check their fruit. They have dry, winged seeds (samaras) that look like canoes. Some say it's because ashes grow near water and their seeds are designed for floating. About 70 species of ash grow in the world; 16 are native to North America. Only one is native to Oregon, although others are planted ornamentally, especially for their bright red fall foliage.

Oregon ash *(Fraxinus latifolia)*

Size: Grows to 80' tall and 3' in diameter.

Leaves: Pinnately compound (5–9 per leaf), opposite, deciduous. Leaflets are roughly elliptical with smooth or very slightly serrated margins.

Fruit: Single samaras that may hang in clusters. Shaped like a canoe.

Twigs: Opposite twigs and buds. Stout.

Bark: Up to 2" thick; grayish-brown; flattened ridges.

Unique leaves. Oregon ash leaves are pinnately compound *and* oppositely arranged on their twigs. These two features occur together in no other native Oregon tree, although they do occur together in elderberry, a large shrub. Oregon ash's pinnately compound leaves have from five to nine leaflets per leaf; each leaflet is broadly elliptical in shape. In addition, the compound leaves arise from opposite sides of the twigs. This feature can be easily determined in any season—from the leaves in summer and from the buds, leaf scars, and twigs in winter.

Fruit, bark, and location. An easy way to identify Oregon ash is by its fruit, which are samaras. Each seed and wing combination is shaped like a canoe. Ash bark is crisscrossed with ridges and resembles a woven net. A medium-size tree, Oregon ash seldom is taller than 80 feet. It likes the plentiful moisture of stream banks, sloughs, and rich lowlands, and is able to survive in heavy clay bottomlands that drain poorly and stay wet for months.

Sportsman's wood. Ash is the sportsman's wood. Baseball bats, oars, skis, and many other kinds of wooden sporting goods are made from ashes native to eastern North America. Oregon ash has a similar wood—hard, tough, and beautiful grain and color—but it's used much less because of its limited availability. However, from time to time it's in strong commercial demand at attractive prices. Look at an ax handle or a wooden baseball bat and notice the wide wood rings. Wide rings indicate rapid growth when the tree was young. Ash wood of this sort is stronger than that from narrow-ring wood and is preferred for the manufacture of sports equipment and tool handles.

Very young trees have better wood

Birches *(Betula)*

Birches are easily recognized by their paperlike bark and distinctive horizontal markings called lenticels. In most species, the bark peels off in thin, papery strips. Another distinctive feature of all birches is their fruit—a papery, disintegrating, cylindrical cone about 1 inch long. Birches are common ornamental trees. There are about 50 species of birch in the world. Eight species reach tree size in North America, and two of these grow in Oregon though their ranges are small and scattered.

Paper birch: bright white bark.

Water birch (sometimes called **red birch**): reddish-brown to black bark.

paper birch *(Betula papyrifera)*

Size: Grows to 70' tall and 2' in diameter.

Leaves: Simple, alternate, deciduous. Egg-shaped; 2–4" long; margins doubly serrate.

Fruit: Tiny, winged nuts borne in a disintegrating cone about 1" long.

Twigs: Slender and droopy.

Bark: White and peeling in horizontal strips. Covered with large, horizontal fissures (called lenticels).

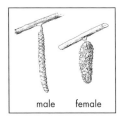

male   female

Unique bark. Bark is the most distinctive feature of paper birch. Although other birches may have whitish bark, none is as pure or peels as easily as that of paper birch. In fact, its very name suggests this feature. Other paper birch features are disintegrating, conelike fruits, typical of all birches, and doubly-serrate leaves with long, tapering tips.

Canoe birch. Although Northwest Indians made their canoes from hollowed-out western redcedar logs, Indians of Canada and the northern United States made theirs from birch bark—peeled in long strips and held together by rawhide laces and sticky, tarlike tree sap. Such canoes carried Indians and early pioneers and adventurers across the continent from the Atlantic to the Rockies. Now, paper birch is used for veneer, pulpwood, and novelties. It's also a common ornamental and shade tree because of its unique bark and graceful appearance.

Where it grows. Paper birch is one of North America's most widespread trees. It grows all across Canada and the northernmost portions of the United States. It just touches the northeast corner of Oregon, where it grows sparingly in the Wallowa Mountains. Many white-bark birches are planted as ornamentals in the Pacific Northwest, but most are native to Europe and Asia and are not paper birch.

water birch *(Betula occidentalis)*

Size: May grow as a shrub or small tree up to 30' tall.

Leaves: Simple, alternate, deciduous. Roundish; 1–2" wide; coarsely serrated; often sticky.

Fruit: Elongated papery cones that disintegrate at maturity. Tiny winged seeds.

Twigs: Slender, droopy, and covered with sticky dots of resin.

Bark: Thin, reddish-brown to coppery; may curl but does not peel.

An apt name. Water birch is common along streams in the mountainous regions of eastern Oregon. It grows most often in clusters 15 to 20 feet tall but may be taller on moist mountain sites.

Caterpillarlike fruits. The fruits of birches—elongated "cones" of papery scales—remind many people of fuzzy caterpillars. Water birch is no exception. Birch fruits fall apart while still hanging from the tree, scattering tiny, winged nutlets far and wide. The seeds are tiny and need to fall on moist, bare mineral soil if they are to survive.

Different from paper birch. Paper birch is noted for its bright white bark; the bark of water birch is reddish-brown or coppery. As a result, it's sometimes called red birch. The leaves of water birch are rounder than those of paper birch and have coarser teeth, resembling the blade of an electric saw. Its twigs are slender and droopy like those of white birch, but they're covered with glistening drops of resin.

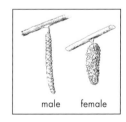

male   female

Buckthorns *(Rhamnus)*

This group of small trees and shrubs has many members—almost 100 worldwide. Only five reach tree size in North America, and only one of those occurs in Oregon. While many of the buckthorns have sharp spines, Oregon's species does not.

cascara buckthorn *(Rhamnus purshiana)*

Size: May grow as a small tree (to 50' tall and 2' in diameter), or an erect shrub (to 15' tall) with multiple stems.

Leaves: Simple, alternate, deciduous. Oblong to elliptical; 2–6" long; smooth, wavy, or finely serrated edges. Prominent, straight veins.

Fruit: Black, cherrylike fruit, ¼–½" in diameter. Inedible.

Twigs: Naked winter buds. Tiny, brown, hairy leaves folded around smaller leaves.

Bark: Thin and grayish with chalky, white patches.

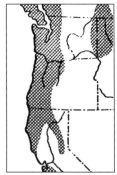

Cascara bud

Cascara = bark. "Cascara" means "bark" in Spanish. The name probably came from early Spanish explorers who learned of the medicinal properties of cascara bark from California Indians. Cascara bark contains a powerful drug used to make laxatives and tonics. The entire world's supply comes from the Pacific Northwest. Synthetic compounds have reduced the demand for bark a bit, but cascara is used in so many drugs all over the world that a steady future demand is predicted. A tree 6 inches in diameter will produce 12 to 15 pounds of dry bark—enough to furnish one dose each to more than 2,000 people.

Naked buds. One detail will positively identify cascara buckthorn—naked winter buds. Other tree buds have an armor of close-fitting scales, but cascara's buds are shielded from winter weather only by a fuzz of rusty brown hairs. The oblong leaves are also distinctive—their veins stick out like ribs. Cascara buckthorn has a smooth, gray bark resembling young alder, but often embellished with chalky white lines and patches. So, cascara is a cinch to recognize: ribbed leaves in summer, naked buds during winter, and gray, splotchy bark throughout the year

Other uses. Grouse, raccoons, and other wildlife often take the cherrylike fruits before we see them. Green or red at first, they ripen to a blue-black. The hard seed inside is not digested, so birds scatter them beside roads and fields and along fence rows. The fruits contain the same chemical as the bark, so generally humans don't eat them.

Understory tree. Cascara buckthorn likes moist locations and deep shade. It mixes with the maples and red alder in western Oregon and reaches a height of 20 to 40 feet with abundant moisture—if it escapes the bark peelers. Cascara has a short trunk that divides into numerous branches to form a rounded head.

Cascara conservation. Cascara buckthorn sprouts vigorously when its top is cut or injured—as long as the entire trunk is not peeled. Therefore, bark peelers will perpetuate their business by cutting down the tree before stripping it, so the stump is not peeled.

California-laurel *(Umbellularia)*

California-laurel is truly unique. There is only one species in the entire genus, so both the genus and species have the same common name—California-laurel. The world's only California-laurel grows along the coast of California and southwestern Oregon. In Oregon, it's commonly called Oregon-myrtle, or myrtlewood. The hyphens in the common names help us remember that this tree is neither a laurel nor a myrtle.

Size: Grows to 100' tall and 5' in diameter. Often has multiple stems and ball-shaped crown.

Leaves: Simple, alternate, evergreen. Pungent odor when crushed. Elliptical to lanceolate; 2–6" long and 1" wide; smooth margins; dark green above and paler green below.

Fruit: Size and shape of a large olive; purple with yellow stalk when ripe; single large seed.

Bark: Smooth and gray-brown when young. Thin, reddish-brown, and scaly when mature.

California-laurel *(Umbellularia californica)*

(often called **Oregon-myrtle**)

Sometimes ball-like

Easy to identify. California-laurel is marked by two unique characteristics: the pungent odor of its leaves, and its olivelike fruit. When bruised, its leaves give off a powerful scent of camphor—the same smell used in many cough drops and medicated jellies. If inhaled deeply, it pains the sinuses, and if rubbed in the eyes, it stings for hours. To overcome chill, Hudson's Bay Company trappers made a tea from the leaves of California-laurel. The fruit of California-laurel is the size and consistency of a large, ripe olive. It has a single, large seed and an outer covering that ranges from purple to black when ripe. The fruit is connected to the twig by a stem that looks like a golf tee.

When in Oregon. California-laurel is commonly known in our state as Oregon-myrtle, or myrtlewood. When grown in the open, it resembles a big pincushion. Its evergreen leaves are shiny and glint brightly in the sun. California-laurel trees often grow in dense, multistemmed clumps, from which two or three trunks will assume dominance and perhaps grow fairly straight in closed stands. On bottomlands, heights of 150 feet and diameters of 5 feet are possible, but on average sites, trees are 40 to 80 feet tall. On harsh sites, they may even grow as tangled shrubs. A superb grove of these trees grows at Loeb State Park near Brookings.

Famous wood. California-laurel wood is marvelous for carving. It's beautiful, is easily worked with tools, and polishes like marble. Dozens of small woodworking shops in western Oregon turn out bowls, clocks, bookends, and other products. In machining qualities, the wood equals the very best American hardwoods and is in demand for furniture, cabinets, paneling, veneer, and gun stocks. Finished myrtlewood is the highest priced of western hardwoods. The big celebration in 1869 that marked completion of the first transcontinental railroad tells us something about the fame of this distinctive wood. The gold spikes were driven into a handsome railroad tie of polished myrtlewood.

Myrtlewood products
are famous

Cherries and Plums *(Prunus)*

Cherry and plum trees belong to a genus that includes apricot, peach, nectarine, and almond trees. Collectively, they're called "stone fruits" because they have fleshy fruits with a single, large seed inside. Two other distinctive features are small glands on the base of the leaf or on the petiole (leaf stalk), and stipules—small, leafy "ears" that appear where the petiole joins the twig. North America contains almost 30 species of this genus, but only three are native to Oregon—two cherries and one plum. It's not uncommon, however, for domesticated cherry trees to "escape" from farms and yards and to find a home in our woods.

Bitter cherry: leaves are elliptical; flowers grow in round clusters; fruits are bright red; bases of leaves often have tiny glands (raised bumps).

Common chokecherry: leaves are oblong to obovate; flowers grow in elongated clusters; petioles often have distinct glands.

Klamath plum: leaves are ovate to oval; flowers grow in round clusters; leaf bases or petioles often have small glands.

bitter cherry *(Prunus emarginata)*

Size: Grows to 50' tall and 18" in diameter.

Fruit: Small, bright red, juicy fruit with a single large seed. Bitter to the taste.

Leaves: Simple, alternate, deciduous. Elliptical; 1–3" long. Glands on base of leaves.

Twigs: Slender; reddish-brown. Spur shoots common on mature twigs.

Bark: Thin; reddish-brown; tends to break and curl horizontally. Large, horizontal lenticels on bark.

Tastes like quinine

Bitter fruit. Most of us relish the sweet taste of commercial cherries, but the bright red fruit of bitter cherries makes us squint and pucker. For this reason, they are considered inedible. The leaves of bitter cherry are narrower than those of most cherries, and their tiny glands are borne on the base of their leaves rather than on their petioles. Their small, white flowers are borne in roundish clusters. Their reddish-brown bark has large, horizontal pores (called lenticels), and it tends to break and curl around the tree

Uses. Deer and elk browse the leaves and twigs, and many birds and mammals delight in the ripened fruit. When the tree grows large enough, its wood is valuable for furniture and gun stocks.

Range. Bitter cherry grows on moist sites throughout most of the western states.

Look here for the projections

Bitter cherry

chokecherry *(Prunus virginiana)*

Size: Large shrub or small tree growing to 30' tall.

Fruit: Small, purple, juicy fruit with a single large seed.

Leaves: Simple, alternate, deciduous. Ovate to elliptical; 2–4" long. Glands usually on petiole.

Twigs: Slender; reddish-brown; smooth. Spur shoots common on older twigs.

Bark: Thin, broken; scaly. Lenticels not present.

Shrubby. Chokecherry is most commonly a shrub but also can grow as a small tree. Its leaves come in a variety of shapes but are generally egg-shaped to elliptical. Its leaf glands typically are on the petiole right below the leaf blade. Its small, white flowers are a good identifying characteristic because they grow in elongated clusters. Its bark is thin and scaly but does not peel as readily as many other cherries, and lenticels are not evident.

Uses. Deer and elk browse its leaves and twigs. Birds and small mammals love its fruit—and so do humans, who gather it for jellies and wine. It's said that the American Indian woman Sacajawea was captured by another tribe while she was gathering chokecherries and was taken east, where Lewis and Clark later found her.

Range. Grows throughout the West but also spans Canada and the northern United States.

Chokecherry

Size: Shrub or small tree growing to 25' tall.

Fruit: Oblong; ½–1" long; yellow, dark red, or purple.

Leaves: Simple, alternate, deciduous. Ovate; about 1–3" long. Glands on petioles or base of leaf.

Twigs: Slender; reddish-brown; conspicuous lenticels. Spur shoots often sharp.

Bark: Grayish-brown; fissured and broken into plates; may be scaly; thin (¼" thick).

Klamath plum *(Prunus subcordata)*

Large fruit. Fruit is perhaps the feature that distinguishes Klamath plum from its closest relatives. Klamath plums are much larger than cherries (½ to 1 inch long) and are oblong. The leaves of Klamath plum are broadly ovate and have small greenish glands either on the petiole or on the base of the leaf. Its flowers are white and are borne in loose, roundish clusters. The bark may be scaly, but does not peel like the bark of many other cherry trees.

Uses. Like its relatives, Klamath plum is browsed by large mammals and its fruit is eaten by a variety of animals, including humans.

Range. Klamath plum likes drier climates than other members of its genus. It ranges from southern Oregon to central California.

Chinkapins *(Castanopsis)*

Chinkapin appears to be an evolutionary link between the oaks and chestnuts. Chinkapin fruits closely resemble those of chestnuts. They are triangular nuts borne inside sharp, spiny burrs. Their twigs resemble those of oaks—with clustered buds and star-shaped piths. There are many species of chinkapin in the world, but only one is native to North America, and it grows in Oregon.

golden chinkapin *(Castanopsis chrysophylla)*

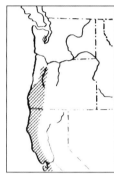

Size: Grows to 150' tall and 6' in diameter. Grows as a shrub at high elevations.

Leaves: Simple, alternate, evergreen. Lanceolate; 2–5" long; stiff and leathery; green above and golden below; smooth margins.

Fruit: Sharp, spiny burr with 1 or 2 triangular nuts.

Twigs: Yellow, star-shaped pith. Terminal buds are clustered.

Bark: Deeply furrowed and ridged; 1–2" thick.

Unique fruit. Golden chinkapin has a light brown, spiny burr that you will not confuse with the fruit of any other Oregon tree. Each burr contains one or two yellowish-brown, triangular nuts that are good to eat. Few humans, however, know their taste for they're guarded as well as if surrounded by porcupines. But chipmunks and squirrels know exactly how to gain entry.

Helpful name. Golden chinkapin's name helps identify it because its leaves are golden underneath. It's so distinctive that you'll know it immediately when you see it, even for the first time. Its leaves are evergreen, leathery, 2 to 5 inches long, and tapered at both ends. Its creamy white flowers continue to bloom throughout the summer and make the tree conspicuous, especially where it's shrubby and the flowers are near eye level. They're arranged in fluffy spikes that stick out stiffly in various directions like the pegs on a clothes tree. They emit a strong, musky odor that hangs in the air with the pervasiveness of a skunk's odor but is less objectionable. The scientific name of the species, *chrysophylla*, means "gold leaf."

Range. Golden chinkapin grows over most of western Oregon below 5,000 feet and at scattered points on the east slopes of the Cascades. In northwest Oregon and in high country, it's a low shrub and frequently grows in thickets. From Benton County south, trees commonly grow to 100 feet

tall and 4 feet in diameter. Looking like ornamentals, the shiny, dense pyramids of chinkapin stand out on forested hills, especially in winter when many other broadleaves are bare. Forest-grown specimens on favorable sites tend to have straight trunks, rather like conifers. Golden chinkapin also grows throughout California.

Uses. Golden chinkapin has excellent qualities for furniture, hardwood plywood, construction lumber, and packaging. However, commercial use is limited by the scattered distribution of large trees.

Cottonwoods, Poplars, and Aspens (Populus)

Members of this group of trees may be called cottonwoods, poplars, or aspens, depending on what species they are. Nonetheless, they're all members of the same genus, *Populus*. Perhaps the most distinguishing feature of this group of trees is their cottony fruits that fill the air and water around them in early spring. Because of this, male trees often are selected for shade and landscaping to avoid the unsightly "cotton" showered all over the place by female trees. The leaves of *Populus* tend to have silvery or white backsides and very long leaf stems, which make it apparent when the wind is blowing through them.

About a dozen members of this genus are native to North America. As a group, they're fast growing, they sprout easily from root suckers and cut branch tips, and they turn bright yellow in fall. Trees within the genus can be crossed readily to form hybrids whose growth characteristics far exceed either of their parents'. As a result, many hybrids are grown in large plantations with an eye toward producing wood fiber for paper.

Three species are native to Oregon, but many others have been planted as ornamentals, as shade trees, and for wind breaks. Oregon's natives include:

Black cottonwood: huge tree; large, triangular leaves with white and bronze undersides.

Quaking aspen: small tree; roundish leaves with white undersides and flat petioles that cause leaves to flutter in the wind; greenish-white bark.

Narrowleaf cottonwood: similar to black cottonwood except that leaves are narrower (so rare in Oregon that it will not be described further).

Size: Grows to 200' tall and 6' in diameter.

Leaves: Simple, alternate, deciduous. Triangular; 3–6" long but sometimes much larger; green above and white below, often with rusty markings. Margins are smooth or with rounded teeth.

Fruit: Round capsules on a string; contain numerous tiny, cottony seeds.

Twigs: Stout. Terminal buds are cigar-shaped, sticky, and smelly.

Bark: Smooth and gray on young trees. Furrowed and ridged on mature trees.

black cottonwood *(Populus trichocarpa)*

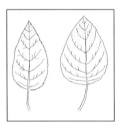

Silvery flashes. Black cottonwood leaves come in two distinct shapes: triangular and spear. Spear-shaped leaves are most common on sprouts arising from roots or the base of the tree. Triangular leaves commonly form higher in the tree's crown. Regardless of the leaves' shapes, their long and sometimes flat petioles cause them to flash their silvery white undersides when stirred by the wind. The flashing that results can be used to identify cottonwoods from quite a distance. There is perfume all around when the long, shiny cottonwood buds open. They're coated with a sweet-smelling, sticky resin, sometimes called balsam, which is responsible for local names of "balm" or "bam."

Tallest broadleaf in western North America. The tall, broadleaved trees lining western Oregon rivers are usually black cottonwoods. Cottonwoods are the tallest, and often broadest, western broadleaved tree. Giants more than 9 feet thick and 200 feet tall once grew along the Columbia River flats. Black cottonwood is also a familiar tree along streams east of the Cascades.

Along the Oregon Trail. To pioneers on the old Oregon Trail, cottonwoods were most important. For nearly a thousand miles of their journey, cottonwoods were the only shade trees to be found. Cottonwoods still help make prairie farms and villages attractive. Although used a little for lumber and excelsior (packing material before Styrofoam nurdles were invented), black cottonwood is always in demand for paper making. In fact, the earliest forest tree plantings in this region were black cottonwoods set out along the Willamette River near Oregon City in 1901 to supply a local pulp mill.

Where it grows. Black cottonwood has a large but winding range. It stretches from southeast Alaska into Baja California and from the Pacific to the Dakotas. But for much of its range, it grows only along rivers and streams, avoiding hot, dry territory.

In the spring, cottonwoods perfume the air

Cottonwoods—there's water and shade

quaking aspen *(Populus tremuloides)*

Size: Small tree growing to 80' tall and 2' in diameter. Short lived.

Leaves: Simple, alternate, deciduous. Ovate to round; 2–3" in diameter; green above and paler below; edges smooth or with rounded teeth. Petioles long and flat.

Fruit: Cone-shaped capsule with cottony seeds.

Bark: Greenish-white when young. May turn dark and furrowed with age.

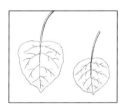

Trunk has nice white color

Widespread. Although quaking aspen is in more states than any other tree, it grows sparingly in Oregon. It grows in our upper Cascades and eastward, especially along mountain streams, on moist slopes, in openings in the woods, and near the edges of mountain lakes and meadows. It also grows beneath pine forests bordering the Oregon high desert. Aspens are scarce in western Oregon.

Easy to learn. A beginner learns aspen almost without trying. The smooth, greenish-white bark has just enough chlorophyll to photosynthesize before the leaves come out in spring. But the leaf has the gimmick that identifies aspen— a flat, flexible leaf stem held at right angles to the leaf blade. The slightest breath of wind sets the leaves dancing. The dainty aspen is conversational; its leaves whisper to the winds. Those same leaves daub the mountains with yellow gold in October. Small wonder it is a popular ornamental.

Disturbance-related species. Aspens are short-lived trees that sprout profusely from their roots when they're injured. Fire plays an important role in maintaining aspen in the forest. When fires are free to burn, many aspens are damaged and send up new, vigorous sprouts. When fire is limited, individual trees soon die and are replaced by more shade-tolerant species. An original tree and its attached sprouts are called a clone—all members are genetically identical to one another. One clone in Colorado is reported to have 47,000 trees attached to the same root, and is considered by some to be the largest single organism in the world.

Important to wildlife. Although the inner bark of aspen is bitter to our taste, it's a favorite of beavers, who store cuttings for winter meals. Many other animals, including livestock, browse the bark, buds, and shoots. Because aspens sprout so easily from their roots, entire stands that have grown above the reach of wildlife can be disked into the ground by giant cutting blades in order to stimulate new growth.

Aspen, Colorado. The mountainsides of central Colorado are so famous for their beautiful stands of aspen that the town of Aspen adopted the tree's name.

Dogwoods (Cornus)

Dogwoods are noted for opposite leaves whose veins turn dramatically toward the apex when they reach the margin and for large, showy flowers. In truth, the showy "petals" are actually white or pink leaves, called bracts, that surround clusters of tiny, densely packed flowers. Of the 45 species of dogwood in the world, 13 are native to North America. Of these, only two species—one tree and one shrub—are native to the Pacific Northwest, although many others have been introduced for ornamental purposes.

Pacific dogwood: grows as a tree; has large, showy "petals" surrounding each flower; branches dip between leaf clusters; fruits are orange to red.

Western dogwood: grows only as a shrub; does not have large, showy "petals" surrounding each flower; branches are straight; fruits are white; twigs are often bright red, giving rise to another common name, red-osier dogwood (will not be further described here).

Pacific dogwood (Cornus nuttallii)

Size: Grows to 60' tall but usually much smaller.

Leaves: Simple, opposite, deciduous. Ovate; 3–5" long; smooth, wavy margins; curved veins. Turn bright red in autumn.

Flowers: Tiny, whitish flowers surrounded by 4 or 6 large, white bracts.

Fruit: Flattened, reddish "berries" in dense clusters.

Twigs: Opposite twigs and buds. Branches dip from leaf cluster to leaf cluster.

Bark: Thin, gray, and smooth.

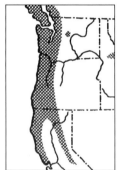

Unique flowers. No one mistakes Pacific dogwood during the flowering season because it has the most brilliant white blooms in our forests. Dogwood flowers are small and inconspicuous, but they're surrounded by a set of large, white, petal-like leaves, called bracts. Four to six of these showy leaves surround each buttonlike cluster of tiny, greenish-yellow flowers. From each cluster of flowers will arise several bright orange to red "berries" to delight birds in fall and winter. Dogwood leaves, like its flowers, are unmistakable. Their veins curve to follow the outline of the leaf—and they turn brilliant red in the fall of the year.

Understory tree. Dogwoods commonly grow 20 to 30 feet tall but may reach 50 feet or more. They can endure shade and grow quite large as understory trees in tall conifer forests west of the Cascades. Old dogwoods have bark that is broken into small, thin scales resembling alligator hide. Pacific dogwoods grow on the west side of the Cascades and Sierras from

British Columbia to southern California; they also grow sporadically in wetter parts of Idaho.

Why dogwood? Skewers, or "dags," once were made from the wood, giving it the name "dagwood" that later became "dogwood." Our species closely resembles the famed eastern dogwood, whose similar heavy, hard wood is used for textile shuttles, golf clubs, and piano keys. Botanist-explorer David Douglas thought Pacific dogwood was the eastern dogwood, but in 1835 Thomas Nuttall found differences in the floral leaves.

Birds like the red berries

Color abounds. Find Pacific dogwood and you find color: white blossoms, clusters of bright red fruit, and fall foliage that runs from green to orange, red, and purple. Dogwoods in bloom are considered by many our most beautiful trees. Nature essayist Ben Hur Lampman spoke of them as white sails on the hill slope. Pacific dogwoods are commonly planted as ornamental trees along our streets and in our yards. However, that practice is slowing as native dogwoods, in both forests and planted settings, are being killed by a rapidly spreading fungal disease called *Anthracnose*. Some species of Asian dogwoods appear resistant to this disease and are being planted instead of native species.

Sometimes blooms twice a year

Hawthorns (*Crataegus*)

Hawthorn is a large, diverse group of trees. Literally hundreds of different species and varieties have been developed for ornamental planting. Two distinctive features of hawthorns are sharp, woody thorns, and small, colorful, applelike fruits. Hawthorns are commonly planted because of their beautiful flowers and colorful fruit.

Two species of hawthorn are native to Oregon, although others have been distributed far and wide by birds and humans. The two Oregon natives are relatively easy to tell from one another when they have fruit but may be difficult at other times.

Black hawthorn: tree or shrub; black fruit; thorns usually shorter than 1 inch.

Columbia hawthorn: grows only as a shrub; red fruit; thorns usually longer than 1 inch; grows on east flank of Cascades and along Columbia Gorge (will not be described further).

black hawthorn *(Crataegus douglasii)*

Size: Small tree (to 30' tall) or thicket-forming shrub.

Leaves: Simple, alternate, deciduous. Egg-shaped; 1–4" long. Margins doubly serrate or lobed and serrate. Commonly have large stipules.

Fruit: Small, black pome (apple) about ¼" in diameter.

Twigs: Short (under 1" long), stiff thorns. No terminal bud. Reddish-brown.

Bark: Thin; shallow fissures to scaly.

Most common native. Black hawthorn, sometimes called Douglas hawthorn or black haw, is Oregon's most common hawthorn. It grows as a small tree or in shrubby thickets that provide important cover for foraging birds and small mammals. It grows along streams, fences, ditches, edges of fields and roads, and in forest openings. It likes moist locations and in eastern Oregon will follow creeks out into the dry country, mixing with other small trees. It ranges from southeast Alaska to central Nevada.

Fruit is the key. Identify black hawthorn by its black fruit and short thorns (commonly shorter than 1 inch). It has egg-shaped leaves with toothed margins that sometimes start to divide into lobes. It has white blossoms and clusters of black, applelike fruits about ¼ inch in diameter. Although Oregon crab apple has similar leaves, it does not have thorns.

Madrones *(Arbutus)*

The madrone genus contains about 20 species of trees and shrubs worldwide. Three are native to North America, but only one grows in the Pacific Northwest. Although peeling bark is the most distinctive feature of Oregon's species, not all species of madrone have this characteristic.

Pacific madrone *(Arbutus menziesii)*

Size: Grows to 100' tall and 6' in diameter.

Leaves: Simple, alternate, evergreen. Oblong; 3–5" long; thick and leathery; dark green above and light green below. Edges smooth or finely serrated.

Fruit: Small (pea size), round, orange-red, berry-like fruit with a pebbly texture.

Twigs: Stout; smooth; may be green, orange, or reddish-brown.

Bark: Flakes off in scales or strips; outer bark is orange or reddish-brown; inner bark may be bright green.

Unique bark. Archibald Menzies, the Scottish botanist who accompanied explorer George Vancouver to British Columbia in 1792, first described Pacific madrone in these words: *"Its peculiar smooth bark of a reddish brown color will at all times attract the notice of the most superficial observer."* Madrone is quickly identified, even from a distance, by its reddish-brown, naked-looking upper stems. A thin outer bark is always peeling off those branches, leaving them smooth and greenish. Old bark is brown and doesn't peel, although it's sometimes flaky. It's sometimes said that madrone sheds its bark instead of its leaves, although the leaves are shed, too, about the middle of their second summer. Pacific madrone is a broadleaved tree, but it's evergreen, with thick, leathery leaves that last throughout the winter. Clusters of orange-red berries appear in the fall, each like a tiny orange. Birds feast on them. Earlier in the growing season, honeybees swarm over showy clusters of white to pink flowers.

Seldom stands straight. Pacific madrone often leans and twists as though seeking a better view of the world. It is popular for gardens and parks despite some bother from its summer-long shedding of leaves and bark.

Attractive wood. Despite an adequate supply of marketable trees and handsome, cherry-colored wood, Pacific madrone sees only limited use because its wood tends to warp and check as it dries. As these problems are solved, madrone will be sought for furniture, paneling, flooring, and specialty uses. Its heavy, dense wood also makes fine fuel.

HERE'S A FEAST

Maples *(Acer)*

Maples constitute one of the largest, most diverse, and most important groups of broadleaved trees in the world. There are about 125 species of maples, most living in China and the Far East. Maples are noted for their leaves, which grow opposite one another and have palmately arranged lobes and veins, and their propellerlike seeds, called samaras.

Thirteen maples are native to North America; three are native to Oregon: bigleaf, vine, and Rocky Mountain maples. Bigleaf maple is a large tree; vine and Rocky Mountain maples usually grow as large shrubs.

Large Tree (single stem; broad crown):

Bigleaf maple: leaves are commonly 6 to 12 inches in diameter (sometimes larger); samaras (helicopterlike fruit) grow at right angles to one another and have fuzzy heads.

Large Shrubs (multiple stems; usually under 25 feet tall)

Vine maple: leaves have five to nine lobes and are commonly 2 to 4 inches in diameter; samaras grow at 180° angles to one another and do not have fuzzy heads.

Rocky Mountain maple: leaves typically have three main lobes and are 2 to 5 inches wide; samaras grow at right angles to one another and do not have fuzzy heads.

bigleaf maple *(Acer macrophyllum)*

Size: Grows to 100' tall and 4' in diameter.

Leaves: Simple, opposite, and deciduous. Very large. Palmately lobed (5 lobes) with the central lobe having a distinct "waist." Long leaf stalk with milky sap.

Fruit: Double samaras in long clusters; samaras joined at right angles; hairy seeds.

Twigs: Buds and branchlets are opposite.

Bark: Grayish or reddish-brown; interlacing ridges and furrows.

Aptly named. Bigleaf maple gets its name from the size of its leaves. They're usually 6 to 12 inches in diameter but can stretch to 15 inches. Of the world's many species of maples, this has the largest leaf. In addition, the leaf stem is almost as long as the leaf and is the only one of the North American maple leaves from which a milky juice can be squeezed. The leaves of bigleaf maple resemble a human hand with the fingers outspread—each leaf has five main lobes, just as the hand has five fingers. The uppermost lobe has a distinct waist—it appears almost as if someone had pulled a belt around its midsection. Typically, two samaras join to form a V, and unlike other maples, the seeds of bigleaf are covered with dense hairs.

Where bigleaf maple grows. Bigleaf maple grows on the west side of the Cascades and Sierra Nevadas from British Columbia through most of California. It prefers moist, well-drained soils and is one of the most common broadleaved trees in the valleys and foothills of its home range. Its leaves are high in base nutrients and play an important role in enriching the soil.

Uses. When grown in the open, bigleaf maple tends to have a stubby trunk and an immense crown. As a result, it's a common native shade tree in western Oregon. It often can be found spreading a carpet of shade over parks and school yards and nestling over backyards like a broody hen. Its tendency to produce huge burls at the base of the tree makes bigleaf maple a prized furniture wood. Burls contain contorted grain patterns and "birds' eyes" that result in striking veneers and novelties. Many burls are exported to Italy and France to be worked by skilled craftsmen. In the fall, bigleaf maple's bright yellow foliage splashes color over hills that tend to be dominated by dark green conifers. Bigleaf maples produce huge crops of seeds each year, and you'll often see squirrels, birds, and other small creatures enjoying a picnic beneath their spreading crowns. Bigleaf maple also makes fine firewood.

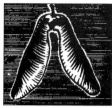

The "key" to maple

"What a big leaf!"

vine maple *(Acer circinatum)*

Size: Generally under 20' tall with multiple stems several inches in diameter.

Leaves: Simple, opposite, deciduous. Palmately lobed with 5–9 lobes (usually 7). Average 2–4" in diameter. Circular outline.

Fruit: Double samaras that resemble an airplane propeller.

Twigs: Opposite buds and branchlets. Twigs often end in 2 buds.

Bark: Smooth with a greenish tinge.

Pinwheels and propellers. Vine maple leaves generally have seven lobes that radiate out from the point where the leaf joins its stalk. When the tips of the lobes are connected in "dot-to-dot" fashion, the leaf resembles a child's pinwheel. Its seeds are easy to distinguish from those of bigleaf—in vine

Bright October color

maple they resemble an airplane propeller. No other tree or shrub in the Northwest woods can match vine maple's glowing fall colors of yellow, orange, and red. They often make the fall woods seem afire.

Where vine maple grows. Look for clumps of stems, usually under 20 feet tall, growing beneath towering conifers like Douglas-fir and western hemlock. Vine maple likes damp places and fairly good soil—prime timber growing sites. It survives heavy shade but also can grow in the full sun. Vine maple grows primarily west of the Cascade crest.

Octopus of the forest. In heavy shade, older vine maples may have long, crooked stems creeping over the ground in search of light. Limbs occasionally root where they touch the ground, sometimes forming an elaborate network of moss-draped arches. To Northwest woodsmen, there is no obstacle course like a vine maple thicket. Pioneer French-Canadian trappers called it "devil wood." Deer and elk have a different opinion—they browse it eagerly—and birds and small mammals love to eat its seeds. When overstory trees are harvested, vine maple can expand rapidly, making reforestation with conifers difficult.

Rocky Mountain maple *(Acer glabrum)*

Size: Generally under 12' tall and several inches in diameter.

Leaves: Simple, opposite, deciduous. Palmately lobed with 3 lobes; margins serrate. Leaves 2–5" in diameter.

Fruit: Double samaras joined at nearly right angles to one another.

Twigs: Opposite buds and branchlets. Buds have 2 dark red scales.

Bark: Smooth with a greenish tinge.

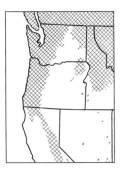

Different leaves. Although Rocky Mountain maple is similar in form to vine maple, its leaves are quite different. Rocky Mountain maple leaves have three main lobes, like the maple leaf on the Canadian penny and flag. Each leaf is 2 to 5 inches across and has serrated margins. The seed and wing are about 1 inch long, and grow in pairs at nearly right angles to one another. Usually Rocky Mountain maple forms a clump of slender stems with up-pointing branches from 10 to 20 feet tall.

Common in eastern Oregon. Rocky Mountain maple is the most common maple of eastern Oregon. Although it grows throughout the state, it's hard to find in the Coast

Range and some other areas. One good place to see it is along roads in the higher country of southern Oregon. This tree seems to like rocky places, canyon walls, and mountain creeks yet often hides in the deep woods. Rocky Mountain maple extends farther east and south than the other Oregon maples, ranging as far east as South Dakota and Nebraska and as far south as New Mexico and Arizona.

Another variety. A variety of Rocky Mountain maple known as Douglas maple (*Acer glabrum* variety *douglasii*) grows occasionally in western Oregon and widely east of the Cascades, stretching north into Alaska. It has shallower leaf indentations than Rocky Mountain maple and nearly parallel seed wings. However, there is so much variation in the leaf shape within the species that the two varieties are difficult to tell apart.

Mountain-mahoganies *(Cercocarpus)*

A tiny, hard seed topped by a feathery tail is one characteristic that clearly separates mountain-mahoganies from other trees and shrubs. Some mountain-mahoganies are deciduous, others are evergreen, and some seem to straddle the line. There are about 10 species of mountain-mahogany, all of which grow only in the western United States. Two species are native to Oregon. The hyphen in the common name alerts us that this group of small trees and shrubs is not related to the true mahoganies that grow in the tropics. It's not uncommon to call a member of this genus by its scientific name, *Cercocarpus*.

Curlleaf mountain-mahogany: small leaves are narrow, tough, and leathery; edges are smooth and curled under. Evergreen.

Birchleaf mountain-mahogany: small leaves are egg-shaped; edges are serrated toward the tip but smooth near the base. Evergreen, but sometimes just barely (old leaves may fall off as new leaves emerge).

Size: An erect shrub to 15' tall or a small tree to 40' tall and 2' in diameter.

Leaves: Simple, alternate (and clustered on spur shoots), evergreen. Elliptical; ½–1" long; thick and leathery; edges curled under.

Fruit: A single seed ½" long with a feathery tail up to 3" long.

Twigs: Spur shoots common.

Bark: Furrows and ridges that break into platelike scales. Red- or gray-brown.

curlleaf mountain-mahogany
(Cercocarpus ledifolius)

(sometimes called curlleaf cercocarpus)

Known by its silver streamer. Curlleaf mountain-mahogany has a silky streamer 1 to 3 inches long attached to each seed, so recognition is easy when fruit is present. Tiny evergreen leaves with margins curled under make identification easy year-round (besides giving curlleaf its name). Curlleaf mountain-mahogany usually is twisted and unshapely because of its struggle with the forces of nature, including browsing animals and a severe climate. Twigs are stiff and almost thornlike. Leaves have a resinous odor.

Where to find it. Look for these tough, shrubby trees growing in scattered groups and tangled thickets across southern Oregon, typically on dry, rocky ridges, in pine forest openings, or scattered across sagebrush flats. Truly a tree of the Southwest, curlleaf ranges from southern Oregon to southern California and east through most of the Rockies.

Uses. The wood of this species has a beautiful mahogany color, taking a high polish. It's very hard and so heavy it will not float. It's a long-burning fuel that gives off intense heat and commonly is used to smoke meats. In some areas, it's an important browse species for deer and elk. Mountain-mahogany often grows in short, dense, tangled stands where many animals find protection both from the weather and from hunters.

birchleaf mountain-mahogany
(Cercocarpus betuloides)

(sometimes called **birchleaf cercocarpus**)

Size: An erect shrub to 15' tall or a small tree to 40' tall.

Leaves: Simple, alternate (and clustered on spur shoots), evergreen (often just barely). Obovate in shape; ½–2" wide; serrated above the midpoint and entire below.

Fruit: A single seed topped by a white, feathery tail up to 3" long.

Twigs: Slender; reddish-brown; spur shoots. Gray to reddish-brown.

Bark: Thin and smooth on young trees, becoming scaly with age.

Resembles curlleaf. Birchleaf mountain-mahogany is similar to curlleaf mountain-mahogany in size and habit but differs in that it has a toothed leaf resembling a small alder or birch leaf. The thick, smooth leaves are more or less evergreen (old leaves may fall off as new leaves emerge in spring, or old leaves may last a second growing season). On young twigs, leaves arise singly, but on older twigs, leaves most often are clustered on spur shoots. The plumed tail attached to the seed is white and 2 to 3 inches long.

Likes the coast. Along the Pacific Coast, birchleaf mountain-mahogany likes the dry foothills and lower mountain slopes of the Coast Ranges and the Sierra Nevadas. But it also grows in the southern Oregon Cascades and southeastward into Arizona.

Uses. Birchleaf mountain-mahogany is browsed by deer and is used by humans for fuel and for turnery items such as bowls and novelties.

Leaves ½" long

Fruit and tail 2" long

Birchleaf mountain-mahogany

Oaks *(Quercus)*

As the lion symbolizes courage, so the oak stands for strength, inspiring the Roman poet Virgil to write nearly 2,000 years ago: *"Full in the midst of his own strength he stands, stretching his brawny arms and leafy hands."*

Oaks make up one of the largest and most diverse groups of trees in the world—with approximately 500 species worldwide and 60 species in North America. Oaks come in all shapes and sizes. Some have huge, wide-spreading crowns, others are small shrubs; some are evergreen, others are deciduous; some grow on very wet sites, others tolerate drought; some have lobed leaves, others are unlobed. Three features that all oaks share are acorns, star-shaped piths (the inner core of the twig), and clusters of large buds at the tips of their twigs.

Fortunately for those of us trying to identify them, only three oaks native to Oregon reach tree size, but many more are planted in lawns and parks throughout the state. Three additional natives grow only as shrubs, but they are merely varieties of the other species and will not be described here.

 Oregon white oak: leaves have rounded lobes; acorns have shallow caps.

 California black oak: leaves have pointed lobes; acorns have deep caps.

 Canyon live oak: small evergreen leaves may have either smooth or spiked edges; acorns have variable caps.

Oregon white oak *(Quercus garryana)*

Size: Grows to 80' tall and 3' in diameter. Has a rounded crown when grown in the open.

Leaves: Simple, alternate, deciduous. Pinnately lobed with 7–9 rounded lobes; lobes often irregular. 3–6" long and 2–5" wide.

Fruit: Acorn with shallow cap; about 1" long.

Twigs: Stout; several buds clustered at tip; fuzzy buds. Pith is star-shaped.

Bark: Grayish; may be shaggy or have shallow ridges and fissures.

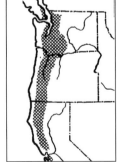

Valley tree. In 1826, explorer David Douglas noted that the low hills of western Oregon were covered by oaks. Today the character and charm of western Oregon's interior valleys are still enhanced by Oregon white oak, but the forests have a different look. The oak–grass savanna lands that Douglas saw were a product of frequent fires set by lightning and by Northwest Indians to improve food for deer and elk. Because of fire suppression over the past 100 years, many of the open oak forests have been taken over by conifers. Despite this, Oregon white oak is still a prominent feature of the interior valleys. Oregon white oak grows throughout the Siskiyou Mountains but seldom ventures west of the Coast Range summit. Only along the Columbia Gorge does it venture into eastern Oregon.

Rounded lobes. Oregon white oak is the only oak native to Oregon with rounded lobes on its leaves, although several introduced species also have this characteristic. Its acorns have a shallow cap, almost like a beret sitting atop a Frenchman's head.

Distinctive form. Before middle age, open-grown trees have a "trimmed" look. A short, stubby trunk will proliferate into a thicket of twisting limbs, sometimes suggesting writhing snakes. In old age, 200 to 500 years, the short, massive trunk and heavy, gnarled limbs are unmistakable. These craggy survivors are scattered in various havens: suburbs, farmsteads, parks, college campuses, and public grounds. They draw our attention, for they're lords of the land—offering us endless visual pleasure. Landscapers like this oak because of its interesting form, tolerance of town conditions, longevity, and deep rooting, which permits garden plants to grow beneath scattered shade trees. Oregon white oaks are intolerant of shade. As a result, when growing in clusters the entire group will assume the shape of a ball, with most of the leaves on the outer surface.

Little used commercially. Oregon white oak has good quality wood suitable for flooring, furniture, ship-building, crossties, and many other uses. It has been little used, however, probably because eastern forests provide ample supplies of oak, and our oaks tend to be scattered and short-trunked. A white oak heartwood post near Eugene lasted for 100 years, showing how durable the heartwood is.

It's strong!

More about white oak. White oak leaves have a protein content nearly equal to alfalfa hay and are browsed by livestock, deer, and other animals. After a disastrous snowfall in 1880, Willamette Valley settlers saved many of their cattle by feeding them white oak twigs and bark. Garry oak is another common name for this tree. Because Nicholas Garry, secretary of the Hudson's Bay Company, helped botanist David Douglas, he is remembered in the scientific name of this species.

Poppers. Each summer, thousands of children delight in stomping the leaves of Oregon white oak—not because they're angry but to pop the large galls that live on the underside. These galls are actually the homes of gall wasps. Don't worry—these wasps do not harm people. They lay their eggs inside oak leaves, and the leaves react by creating a hard,

brittle covering that protects the wasps in their larval stage. In mid to late summer, a heavily infested oak grove may rattle with the sound of the larvae trying to break out of this protective covering.

California black oak *(Quercus kelloggii)*

Size: Grows to 80' tall and 3' in diameter, but usually is smaller.

Leaves: Simple, alternate, deciduous. Pinnately lobed with 7 pointed and bristle-tipped lobes.

Fruit: Acorn with deep cap; 1–2" long.

Twigs: Stout, with buds clustered near the tip.

Bark: Dark with irregular plates; about 1" thick.

Spine-tipped lobes

Pointed lobes. Sharply pointed and bristle-tipped leaves of California black oak distinguish it from other West Coast oaks. However, *many* nonnative oaks that resemble California black oak have been planted in towns throughout the Pacific Northwest. In addition to pointed leaves, look for acorn caps that cover over half the nut (the caps of most other oaks are shallower). Viewed at a distance, California black oaks often resemble maples because of their rounded crowns and shiny, dark green leaves with pointed lobes. This tree seldom grows straight but leans like a sailor who has not found his "land legs." The common name refers to the very dark bark of older trees.

Where to find it. As its name implies, California black oak is most common in California, but it grows as far north as the Umpqua Valley in Oregon. Douglas, Josephine, and Jackson counties contain nearly all the black oaks in Oregon. California black oaks like sun and thrive where it's warm and dry, especially on lower hills and on broad valley bottoms.

Food locker. Acorn woodpeckers do a curious thing to this tree (and to other oaks). They drill holes in the bark just the right size to hold acorns and then hammer them in. That way squirrels can't get them. Many such "food lockers" are seen in oak trees of southwestern Oregon—not to mention in telephone poles, barns, and house siding! Acorns are also a favorite food of other birds and mammals and were eaten by humans in earlier days, after being soaked in water to remove some of the tannin.

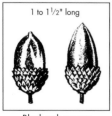

1 to 1½" long

Black oak acorns

Uses for black oak. Today, black oak is used primarily for firewood. But it has possibilities for flooring, furniture, hardware, and other products. Although shorter lived than Oregon white oak, black oak tends to develop rot with age.

canyon live oak *(Quercus chrysolepis)*

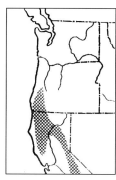

Size: May be a shrub to 15' tall or a tree to 80' tall and 2' in diameter.

Leaves: Two distinctive types on same plant. All are simple, alternate, evergreen; 1–4" long. Some have smooth edges while some are spiked like holly leaves.

Fruit: Acorn from ½–2" long. Cap is variable.

Twigs: Slender; buds clustered at tips. Pith is star-shaped.

Bark: Grayish-brown and scaly. Thin (about 1" thick).

Split personality. Canyon live oak has a split personality. Two kinds of leaves grow on the same tree; one looks like holly, the other has smooth edges. The younger the tree, the more hollylike leaves it will have.

What's in a name? This tree's name tells us something important about it. Live oak refers to the fact that it's evergreen. Canyon refers to the fact that it likes to grow on canyon sides and bottoms, especially those that are hot and dry.

Where it grows. Where it has favorable soil and moisture, canyon live oak may reach 80 feet up. Like most other trees, it assumes a shape according to the space in which it has to grow. The live oaks of the southeastern United State are celebrated for their wide, spreading crowns. When growing in the open on good ground, canyon live oak remembers the family habit—it's broad of crown and short of trunk. Most, however, grow in rough, dry country where they appear as small trees or bushes.

Tough wood. One of the local names for this tree is "maul oak" because farmers and loggers once sought the extremely heavy, tough wood to make mauls. The wood also was used for wagon axles and wheels. Canyon live oak is not commercially valuable at present. Dense, shining foliage and attractive form recommend it as an ornamental, especially in dry regions of the state.

Believes in variety

Tanoaks *(Lithocarpus)*

Tanoaks are an evolutionary link between the oaks and the chestnuts. Tanoaks resemble oaks because they have acorns for fruits, but their acorns have spiny caps reminiscent of the chestnuts. Although there are about 100 species of tanoak in the world, only one is native to North America, and it is in Oregon. Because tanoak is not a true oak, its name is written as one word rather than two.

tanoak *(Lithocarpus densiflorus)*

Size: Grows to 100' tall and 3' in diameter, but also may be shrubby.

Leaves: Simple, alternate, evergreen. Thick and leathery; 3–5" long; bluish-white fuzz underneath; margins smooth or toothed.

Fruit: Acorns with spiked caps.

Twigs: Stout; buds clustered at tips; star-shaped pith.

Bark: Thin with flattened ridges or plates.

Densiflorus: "densely flowered"

Lithocarpus: "Rock fruit" (the fruit is very hard)

Lithocarpus densiflorus

Unique hat. Tanoak has an acorn cap that is really different—and a sure means of identifying the species. Bristles stick out around the cap, similar to the crown on the Statue of Liberty. A leaf also will identify tanoak, and you can always get one because tanoak is evergreen. Mature leaves are thick and leathery and commonly have a bluish-white fuzz on their underside. The veins on their surface are uniformly spaced and create a washboard appearance. Their edges typically, but not always, have widely spaced teeth.

Variable growth form. Tanoak can be tall and narrow in closed stands or short-trunked and spreading in open situations. Shrubby forms climb high into the Siskiyou Mountains. Tanoak is a vigorous, competitive grower in the coastal fog belt, readily attaining 3 feet in diameter and 100 feet in height. When the main stem is cut, buds at the base of the trunk will develop into new trees at an amazing rate. If the tree is killed by fire, new sprouts will arise from underground burls.

Concentrated in Curry County. Tanoak is one of the four most abundant Oregon hardwoods, and 85 percent of its timber volume lies in Curry County. It grows only in southwestern Oregon and California, from sea level to about 5,000 feet.

Uses. Tanoak is fine for plywood, flooring, furniture, and paper making. So far, industrial use has been small, but it could develop—the raw material is there. The bark once had an important industrial use in tanning leather—hence the name tanoak, or tanbark oak. Many Northwest Indian communities subsisted chiefly upon salmon and tanoak acorns. Acorns were ground, leached, and then prepared as a soup, a cooked mush, or a kind of bread. A tree 30 inches thick can produce about 1,000 pounds of acorns yearly.

Once used in tanning

Willows *(Salix)*

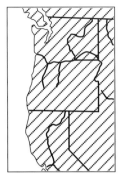

As a group, willows are easy to identify. In fact, pussy willows are one of the first trees many of us learn. But distinguishing between different types of willows is a different story.

The reason is that there are so many willows—North America has approximately 90 different types—and that many of the species interbreed, with the offspring having characteristics of both parents. As a result, most people are satisfied knowing that a tree is a willow and leave it at that.

Form and location are important. All North American willows grow as shrubs, but perhaps a dozen also grow to tree size. Regardless of their size, they typically have a shrubby form, with multiple stems and indistinct crowns. Willows grow almost everywhere but are found most commonly along streams and on wet ground. Some even grow near treeline as prostrate shrubs.

Leaves. Although not all willow leaves are identical, they have a particular look about them—almost like children in the same family. They tend to be narrow and pointed, and are generally yellow-green on top and white below. As a result, wind moving through the willows makes them flutter. They all have short petioles (leaf stalks) and most have leafy "ears" (stipules) where the leaves joins the twigs.

Flowers and fruit. Who has not collected "pussy willows," the earliest harbingers of spring? Willows bear male and female flowers on separate plants, so some flowers will turn into tear-shaped fruits filled with cottony seeds, and others will simply wilt and fall from the plant. The cottony seeds are distributed both by wind and water. Regardless, they are very tiny and need to land on moist soil soon after being dropped or they will dry out and die.

Buds and twigs. Willows can be readily distinguished from other trees by narrow winter buds that hug the twig. Each bud is covered by a single caplike scale that resembles a hood or stocking cap pulled down over it. There is never a terminal bud on willows; the twigs simply die back to a lateral bud in winter. Willow twigs are

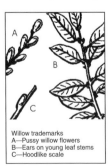

Willow trademarks
A—Pussy willow flowers
B—Ears on young leaf stems
C—Hoodlike scale

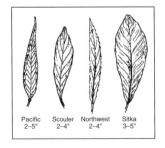

Pacific 2–5" Scouler 2–4" Northwest 2–4" Sitka 3–5"

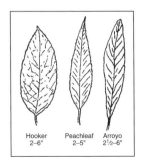

Hooker 2–6" Peachleaf 2–5" Arroyo 2½–6"

often yellowish-green, sometimes with tinges of purple or red. Have you ever noticed a vivid yellow or red haze hanging over creeks or gullies in late winter? It's likely to be the colorful stems of willows reminding us that spring is near. These showy willow thickets are especially common east of the Cascades.

Uses of willows. Willows of our region do not typically reach commercial size, yet they perform great service in reducing stream bank erosion because of their clinging roots and tangled branches. Baskets made from long, supple willow twigs were probably among the earliest manufactured products of humans. Now, willow twigs are used to make unique lawn furniture, and the tough, springy wood is used to make croquet balls and cricket bats. Introduced species such as weeping willow and golden willow are common shade and ornamental trees. Many species of wildlife like to eat the twigs and flowers of willows. Rabbits, mice, beaver, grouse, and a host of other wildlife eat willow bark; deer and livestock browse stems. While we may not always notice the willows, other eyes do not overlook them.

Willows are everywhere. If you are camping, remember to look for willow wood along lakes and streams. It's an even-burning, superior wood for fires and camp stoves. Willow is short lived, so dead trees or limbs are always available. Willows may be small and humble, but they grow abundantly where animals gather, as all must have water. Willows stand water as well as any tree known and even grow well on poorly drained land. They sprout easily from stumps and even from pieces of branch or root that break off from the parent plant and are buried in the soil.

Oregon's Tree-size Willows

Scouler willow (*Salix scouleriana*)—probably the most common willow in western North America. It grows not only at low elevations but on higher mountains. In western Oregon, it often reaches 40 feet tall. Unlike other willows, it thrives away from water. It's also called mountain willow.

Pacific willow (*Salix lasiandra*)—a black-barked tree or large shrub found around wet places. It often reaches 40 to 60 feet tall and is abundant west of the Cascades at low and moderate elevations. Identification is aided by two or more tiny nodules at the base of each leaf blade. It's also called black willow.

Peachleaf willow (*Salix amygdaloides*)—found along streams and around farm homes in extreme northern and eastern Oregon. This is the largest willow east of Cascades, sometimes reaching 70 feet tall.

Hooker willow (*Salix hookeriana*)—a beach willow found the full length of the Northwest coast and seldom more than 5 miles from salt water. Its location and wide leaf improve chances of identification. It can be found along streams and on swampy ground, near sea level.

Northwest willow (*Salix sessilifolia*)—has long, narrow leaves, often 10 times as long as they are wide. It grows in western Oregon south to the Klamath Mountains and is sometimes called sandbar willow.

Sitka willow (*Salix sitchensis*)—grows mainly west of the Cascades, with scattered appearances in eastern Oregon, especially in the Wallowa Mountains. Some leaves have a pear-shape outline. It's also called silky willow because of satiny hairs on the undersides of its leaves.

Oregon's Principal Urban Trees

(Ornamental, Shade, and Fruit Trees)

Though most of the trees inhabiting our forests are "native Oregonians," most of the shade, fruit, and ornamental trees that grace our lives are not. Hundreds of species of trees have been introduced from elsewhere in the United States and from foreign lands. Because these are the trees that dominate our yards, streets, and public grounds, they're often interwoven more closely with our daily lives than are our native trees.

This section describes some of Oregon's most common and important imported trees, but by no means all of them. Because Oregon's climate permits all but the most tropical of trees to thrive here, a complete list would be long indeed! Therefore, we've selected trees you're most likely to see, but we do not mean to imply that these are more important than others you might find.

Trees within this section are listed alphabetically by the common name of their genus. Most can be identified by using the keys that appear earlier in this book.

Common Introduced Conifers

Arborvitae: several species (*Thuja* spp.)

Many of Oregon's most beautiful hedges are formed from this adaptable evergreen conifer. Though there are many species of arborvitae, all are related to our native western redcedar. Like redcedar, they all have scalelike leaves and small, upturned cones that resemble woody rosebuds. Many varieties grow tall and slender and can be pruned into a variety of forms—good attributes for hedges.

Cedars or "true" cedars: several species (*Cedrus* spp.)

True cedars are native to the Middle East and are very different from the scale-leaved false cedars native to Oregon. True cedars have evergreen needles borne in dense clusters on stout, woody pegs (similar to larches). Their large, barrel-shape cones stick up above their branches and have thin scales that fall apart when mature (similar to true firs). Three true cedars commonly are planted in Oregon:

Deodar cedar (*Cedrus deodara*): the largest, most common, and easiest to recognize of the true cedars. Its needles are 1 to 2 inches long and are yellow-green to blue-green. Needles are borne in dense clusters on large, woody pegs except near the tips of branches, where they're borne individually. Branch tips and the leader droop noticeably, similar to western hemlock. Deodar cedar is native to the Himalayan Mountains of northern India.

Atlas cedar (*Cedrus atlantica*): similar to Deodar cedar except that it has shorter needles (about 1 inch long) and slightly smaller cones (2 to 3 inches long). In addition, its needles have a blue-green color and a white bloom. Atlas cedar is named for the Atlas Mountains of northern Africa. Also called Atlantic cedar.

Cedar of Lebanon (*Cedrus libani*): nearly identical to Atlas cedar. Both exhibit a stiff branching habit and have blue-green needles about 1 inch long. Cedar of Lebanon has slightly larger cones (3 to 4 inches long). This tree is native to Asia Minor and reportedly was used to build King Solomon's temple.

Cypress: many species (*Cupressus* spp.)

Cypresses are attractive evergreen conifers that come in a variety of shapes, sizes, and colors. Their scalelike foliage resembles that of the false cedars (except that the smallest sprays of cypress tend to be rounded rather than flat), and the junipers (except that cypresses commonly do not have sharp-pointed needles). Their round cones resemble those of Port-Orford- and Alaska-cedars, although cypress cones are much larger (often over ½ inch in diameter.)

Giant sequoia: giant sequoia
(*Sequoiadendron giganteum*)

Giant sequoias are the largest trees ever to live on earth and are among the oldest. Heights of 300 feet and diameters of 30 feet are not uncommon. Their ages commonly range from 2,000 to 3,000 years (only bristlecone pines are older). Although once widespread, giant sequoias now grow only in the Sierra Nevada Mountains of central California. In olden times, it took days for a team of men to fell one tree, and then dances were held on the stump; a roof over a stump made a comfortable home for many settlers; and an entire cavalry unit once spent the night inside a burned-out log—with their horses! Since 1890, giant sequoias have been protected in Yosemite, Kings Canyon, and Sequoia national parks as well as in smaller individual groves. Giant sequoias' great age and size place them in a lofty world of their own, similar to the Greek gods who dwelt on Mount Olympus apart from humans. These stately trees induce awe, humility, and reverence in people who stand in the dim light below them.

The leaves of giant sequoia are short, thick, and sharp-pointed—unlike the leaves of any other American tree. Cones are about the size of a hen's egg (2 to 3 inches long) and are nearly as hard as a rock. The bark is reddish-brown, stringy, and very thick—good protection from insects, disease, and fire. Through middle age, giant sequoias have a nearly perfect conical shape.

Spruce: Colorado blue spruce
(Picea pungens)

Although many spruces are planted as ornamentals throughout Oregon, Colorado blue spruce is by far the most common because of its striking blue foliage. A native of the central and southern Rockies, this tree resembles our native Engelmann spruce except for its bluer foliage. The needles of Colorado blue spruce are about 1 inch long, are four-sided, and are stiff and sharp; most have a distinct blue color, although some are green. As with all spruces, each needle is borne on its own woody peg.

Yew: English yew (Taxus baccatta)

Its dark green foliage and bright red fruit make English yew a commonly used conifer for hedges and ornamentals. Its ability to be pruned makes it a favorite for topiary. English yew greatly resembles its cousin, Pacific yew, except that English yew has a much more vigorous, healthy growth form. Fruits and leaves are highly toxic to humans but can be eaten by birds without harm. Like Pacific yew, English yew produces taxol, which is being used in the fight against some types of cancer.

Common Introduced Broadleaved Trees

Apple, pear, and crab apple: many species *(Pyrus* spp.)
(Apples and crab apples sometimes are called Malus *spp.)*

Apple: the leading fruit tree in Oregon and the nation. Earliest recorded history calls apples the "gift of the gods." Apple trees are easily identified by their characteristic round fruit known technically as a *pome*—a fleshy fruit having seeds borne within papery cells at the core. There are many species of apple trees and several thousand varieties. Apple leaves are oval, mostly pointed at the tip and rounded at the base, soft in texture, and dull in color. The large, showy flowers are borne in clusters. Apple seeds are spread by animals and birds so that trees frequently escape to fence rows, abandoned fields, and even cutover forest land.

Crab apple: actually just a wild form of domesticated apples. As a result, crab apple trees resemble common apples except in size. They're usually stiff, low branching, and have multiple trunks. From the great number of varieties have come some of the most valuable ornamental trees in use today. Their branches are wreathed in blooms (white to red) so thick the foliage cannot be seen. Leaves may range in color from bright green to red or purple. Crab apple fruits are small and inedible, but in some cases they provide red, orange, or yellow colors. Birds love them, especially in winter when other food is limited.

Pear: like apple trees, pear trees are travelers, coming to us from western Asia and China. They commonly grow strong and upright, sometimes reaching 50 feet or more. Pear leaves are oblong, borne on short spurs, hard in texture with prominent veins, and have a bright green color. Pear fruit varies in shape from round to oblong but, like apples and quince, has an inner core containing brown seeds. White flowers appear in dense clusters and are attractive enough that nonfruiting varieties are planted as ornamentals. Over 1,000 varieties have been named, but only half a dozen are grown commercially. Oregon is a leading producer of pears.

Basswood: several species
(*Tilia* spp.)

North Americans call this tree "basswood," but others call it "linden." Basswoods are easily recognized by their unique "ribbon leaf," from which hangs a cluster of hard, pea-size fruits. White flowers produce a fragrant nectar that attracts bees. Basswoods have heart-shaped leaves with uneven bases and are about 4 to 6 inches long. It's not uncommon for basswood leaves to have bright red spires on the upper leaf surface, a result of insects' laying their eggs inside the leaf.

Birch: several species (*Betula* spp.)

Several different species of white-bark birches are marketed together under the name of European white birch. The differences between them are minor. Most have bright white bark similar to our native paper birch, but none peels to the same extent. All have typical birch fruits—long, papery cones that disintegrate at maturity. Most have droopy branches that drop resin on anything that's under them. All are popular ornamental trees and tend to be planted in clumps.

Buckeye: several species
(*Aesculus* spp.)

Two common names for the same tree: buckeye because its reddish-brown seed with a huge white dot looks like a buck's eye; and horse-chestnut because its fruit is so similar to American chestnut. Ohio's nickname, the Buckeye State, comes from a common eastern species. All buckeyes have large, palmately compound leaves, the only common tree in North America to have this characteristic. The large brown nuts are packaged in a leathery husk that may or may not have spiny bristles. These husks split open cleanly, along straight lines. The flowers range from white to deep pink, resemble the head of an elephant, and come in huge, upright clusters, making this one of our most spectacular ornamental trees. The fruits are not edible by humans.

Catalpa: two species (*Catalpa* spp.)

Catalpas are noted for their spectacular summer flower displays. Their white, trumpet-shaped flowers grow in huge, upright clusters covering the entire tree. Each flower has a yellow nectar guide to help bees find their pollen; when the pollen is gone, the nectar guide turns red and becomes invisible to bees. From the flowers develop long, thin pods resembling 12- to 18-inch-long string beans. Catalpa leaves are also spectacular: huge and heart-shaped. Both catalpas are native to the southeastern United States.

Cherry, peach, plum, apricot, almond: many species (*Prunus* spp.)

Because of the commercial importance of each of its members, this genus has several common names, depending on which member is under consideration. For this reason, it's often easiest to use the scientific name, *Prunus*, when referring to the entire genus.

Cherry: commonly grown for both the flowers and the fruit. Numerous varieties are available; some are hard to distinguish from one another. Cherry flowers are showy, creamy white to deep rose, and are borne in dense clusters. Some are fragrant, others are not. Some have a single ring of petals, others have multiple rings. Fruits may be red, yellow, or black; and round, heart-shaped, or pointed. Some are delectable, others are bitter. The bark of many cherry trees is thin, reddish-brown, and peels away from the trunk in horizontal strips. Branches have spur shoots and prominent lenticels (pores). Japanese flowering cherry trees are widely planted in Oregon. Their breathtaking flower displays are as eagerly anticipated along our streets as they are in Washington, DC, where a gift of 2,000 cherry trees was received in 1912 from Tokyo, Japan.

Plum: some are grown for their fruit, others for their flowers and foliage. Plum trees come from three continents: Europe, Asia, and America. They have attractive white or pink flowers borne in dense clusters. Fruits range in color from almost black through shades of red, purple, blue, green, yellow, and white. Plum trees commonly have finely toothed leaves with small glands on their petioles; some varieties have thorns. Our best known eating plum is the Italian prune plum, although many others are grown. Several types of flowering plum trees are grown in Oregon, especially 'Pissardi' and 'Bliriana,' noted for their pink flowers and purple leaves.

Peach: introduced to America from China in the 16th century. The tree is twiggy with slender limbs. The pink flowers are solitary and appear before the leaves. Peach trees are shorter (generally under 20 feet) and rounder than apple and pear trees. Dozens of varieties are known, including red-, yellow-, and white-fleshed types; some have purple leaves and double flowers and are planted as ornamentals. The nectarine is a smooth-skinned relative of the peach.

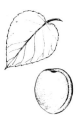

Apricot: similar to other members of the genus, but the trees can be distinguished by broad, sharp-pointed leaves and round, bright yellow fruits. The flowers are about 1 inch across, are pink to nearly white, and appear very early each spring. The flesh of the fruit breaks free from the inner stone, which is flattened and smooth.

Almond: at first glance, the fruit of this tree does not seem to fit its genus. Its outer covering is a hard, green husk, equivalent to the fleshy part of a cherry or plum. Inside is a double-layered seed, equivalent to a cherry or plum "pit." The outer part is semiwoody and filled with holes; this is the part we crack and throw away. Inside is a meaty seed—the almond we eat.

Chestnut: American chestnut
(Castanea dentata)

This native of the eastern United States grows to over 100 feet tall and has leaves up to 10 inches long. The leaves have slender points on the teeth, often curving inward. They are more than three times as long as they are wide and are green on both sides. Two to four smooth, brown nuts are found inside a very prickly burr, which breaks open around Halloween. The sweet, edible nuts must be roasted for maximum enjoyment. Although the chestnut was once a dominant tree in eastern forests, a virulent blight swept through the forests in the early 1900s, killing nearly every chestnut tree in its path. As a result, American chestnuts are no longer commonly planted, although a great deal of research is taking place to try to reestablish the species.

Dogwood: pink flowering dogwood *(Cornus florida)*

Many dogwoods are now planted in Oregon. Perhaps the most common is pink flowering dogwood, a native of the southeastern United States. This species is actually a variety of a white-flowered eastern species similar to Pacific dogwood, different only in its pink, petal-like bracts. Several Oriental dogwoods have gained favor recently because they're more resistant to a root rot that kills native dogwoods.

Elm: American elm *(Ulmus americana)*

A large tree of unforgettable form, American elm resembles the spray of a fountain, or a bursting skyrocket. It grows naturally throughout the eastern United States and is especially prominent in the lovely old towns of New England. American elms once were planted in most western Oregon cities but seldom are planted anymore because they're susceptible to Dutch elm disease, which is almost always lethal. The same disease has killed a vast number of American elms in the eastern part of the country. Know American elm by its form; its lopsided, double-toothed leaf; and its flat, gauzy-winged fruit—the original "flying saucer." Several other elms, especially Chinese and Siberian elms, are grown in Oregon.

Hawthorn: many species *(Crataegus spp.)*

Hawthorns, also called haws or thornapples, are the only trees with both conspicuous thorns and leaves that are lobed and serrated. The flowers are like small roses, followed by clusters of small, apple-like fruits, or haws. Haws are edible but quite seedy. This group grows throughout the world and includes a vast number of species and varieties. Oregon has two native species, Columbia and black hawthorn. Most common of the cultivated haws is English haw. The leaf usually is five-lobed, and its flowers may be pink, red, or white. Birds spread its seeds almost everywhere.

Hazel: filbert *(Corylus avellana)*

The filbert is a close relative of our native California hazel. It's a small, deciduous tree easily recognized both in winter and summer. In winter it bears long, male catkins that shed yellow pollen between December and March. Female flowers resemble a large bud with several red whiskers sticking out from the end. "Filbert" is supposed to mean "full beard," referring to the husk covering the nut. Dozens of varieties are known. Nuts vary in shape from round to oblong and from ¼ to 1 inch in diameter. Each nut is enclosed in a leafy "basket" called an involucre. Oregon produces 99 percent of the nation's filbert crop, marketing them as hazelnuts.

Holly: several species *(Ilex spp.)*

Holly trees are beautiful and long lived. They grow on all continents except Australia, with hundreds of species, hybrids, and varieties. In Oregon, the most common species is English holly, *Ilex aquifolium*, which is grown in commercial orchards for the production of Christmas sprays and wreaths. Hollies also are widely planted as ornamentals. They are easy to identify by spike-tipped, shiny, evergreen leaves, and bright red berries, frequently deposited by birds in hedges and along fences. Holly bears male and female flowers on separate trees. English holly ranges from 20 to 40 feet tall; branches extend to the ground. Variegated forms are available with white or silver margins or even with smooth-edged leaves. Roman Christians apparently started the custom of decorating with holly for Christmas, but holly was used long before in pagan rites.

Honeylocust *(Gleditsia triacanthos)*

Honeylocust has pinnately and doubly-pinnately compound leaves—meaning it may have a double set of compound leaves arising from the same leaf stalk. In addition, it has long, brown seed pods that are flat and twisted so the wind can roll them across the ground. Inside are hard, shiny brown seeds that shake like rattles when the pods are ripe. Some honeylocusts have huge, sharp, multiple-pointed thorns, but most ornamentals have been bred not to have them. Honeylocusts are native to the eastern United States. Trees are fast growing with an upright trunk and spreading branches, making them a favorite shade tree.

Locust: black locust
(Robinia pseudoacacia)

Settlers took black locust all over the United States because they loved the fragrant, sweet-pea flowers and because of its tolerance of harsh growing conditions. A native of the southern Appalachian and Ozark highlands, black locust has been planted throughout Oregon, especially on the east side of the Cascades where its resistance to heat, cold, and drought is useful. Black locust is distinguished by pinnately compound leaves; two short, wicked spines at the base of each leaf; and flat, brown seed pods. Young leaves, when seen in the sunlight, are said to show the most beautiful green of any broadleaf. Black locust grows rapidly to a height of 75 feet and is used in windbreaks. Its wood can provide very durable posts, even without treatment.

Black locust "fixes" nitrogen from the air and is, therefore, often used to help replenish the soil brought to the surface during strip mining.

Maple: many species (Acer spp.)

Dozens of species of maple thrive in the mild climate of western Oregon. Only a few will be mentioned here. All maples have opposite leaves and dry-seeded fruits shaped like airplane propellers (samaras).

Norway maple *(Acer platanoides)*: a native of Europe that shades many Oregon streets and lawns. It resembles our native bigleaf maple, but neither its leaves nor its size are nearly as large. Norway and bigleaf are the only maples whose leaf stems contain milky juice. Schwedler's maple, a smaller variety of Norway maple, has rich, dark red leaves that make it an important ornamental.

Silver maple *(Acer saccharinum)*: a widely planted shade tree native to the eastern United States. Its leaves are cut with deep indentations and show a silvery-white color underneath. Silver maple has a wide-spreading form with the trunk dividing near the ground into big, mostly upright limbs. It's rapidly growing but short lived. It tends to shed dead branches more easily than other maples and is subject to damage from ice, wind, and snow.

Red maple (*Acer rubrum*): native to the eastern United States. They are widely planted shade trees because of rapid growth, uniform shape, and leaves that turn brilliant red in the fall. They are easy to distinguish from other maples because their leaves have only three lobes.

Japanese maples: actually a large group of trees widely planted as ornamentals because they come in a variety of sizes and shapes. Their leaves are also different: most often deeply lobed and star-like. As with all maples, their leaves are opposite, and their fruits are samaras.

Mountain-ash: many species and varieties *(Sorbus spp.)*

Although one species of mountain-ash grows at high elevations in Oregon's mountains, it's a shrub rather than a tree. However, many nonnative species do grow as small tress—and they're commonly chosen to adorn our streets and yards. Mountain-ashes are popular ornamentals because of their vibrant colored fruits—red, yellow, and orange. The small, applelike clusters are a favorite of birds and small mammals, especially in winter when other food is scarce. Mountain-ashes also have the ability to grow in tight spaces, making them a favorite for storefronts and shopping centers. The hyphen in the common name tells us this is not a true ash.

Oaks: many species *(Quercus spp.)*

Many species of oaks have been introduced into Oregon as shade and ornamental trees. Most are classified as red oaks because their leaves have pointed lobes ending in several bristle tips. Those with rounded lobes and no bristle tips are called white oaks. All oaks have acorns.

Northern red oak (*Quercus rubra*) and scarlet oak (*Quercus coccinea*): both are native to the eastern United States and are so similar that identification is difficult. Both are large, open-growing trees that sport blazing red fall colors. Their leaves are 3 to 6 inches long and have five to nine bristle-tipped lobes. Although the leaves of each species are quite variable, those of scarlet oak tend to have deeper lobes than those of northern red oak.

Pin oak *(Quercus palustris)*: a large oak of the eastern United States that can be recognized by its outline alone. Its upper branches point up, its middle branches spread horizontally, and its lower branches droop until they sweep the ground. Short, pinlike shoots cluster along the branches, giving the tree the name of pin oak. We see this tree rather often in Oregon. The glowing red-bronze autumn foliage and handsome winter form are especially attractive. It tends to hold dead leaves well into winter. Pin oak has deeply cut leaves, 3 to 5 inches long. The acorns, ½ inch long, are topped by flat caps.

Oleaster: Russian-olive
(*Elaeagnus angustifolia*)

Russian-olive is a small, bushy tree, sometimes spiny, that is commonly planted in rural districts of eastern Oregon. It's popular for its handsome, silvery foliage, fragrant, pale-yellow flowers, fast growth, and adaptability to a wide range of conditions. Its leaves are 1 to 3 inches long and have silvery, scaly undersides; its fruit is small, one-seeded, and mealy. Leaves, twigs, flowers, and fruits are all touched with silver.

Poplar: Lombardy poplar
(*Populus nigra* var. *italica*)

Lombardy poplar is easily identified by its slim, columnar shape—like an exclamation point rising from the landscape. Close up, you can note its up-pointing branches and triangular leaves with slender, flattened leaf stalks, making them "fluttery." Lombardy poplars are all male trees—that is, they do not produce seeds. Instead, they're propagated only by cuttings, a process that results in genetically identical "clones." Because of their narrow growth form and similar growth rates, Lombardy poplars are frequently used for tall hedges and windbreaks.

Sweetgum *(Liquidambar styraciflua)*

Sweetgum is an ornamental that comes to Oregon from the southeastern United States. It's easily identified by its five- to seven-pointed leaves that suggest stars. Two other features that help identify it: twigs that develop thick, corky ridges, and fruit that

is a peculiar, spiny ball about the size of a golf ball that hangs on the tree well into winter. When fall weather is favorable, sweetgum's parade of color is unsurpassed. We say "parade" because one bright color follows another—scarlet, orange, wine, yellow, brown, and purple. Entire streets in western Oregon are lined with sweetgums to take advantage of their many attributes.

Sycamore: several species
(*Platanus* spp.)

In North America, trees in this genus are called sycamores, but in the rest of the world they're called planetrees. Several species are planted in Oregon as street and shade trees, but they're similar enough to be described together. Sycamores are easy to recognize because they shed their greenish-gray outer bark to reveal chalky, light patches of inner bark, and because their fruits are 1-inch balls of tiny, tufted seeds that hang on long threads. Sycamores are sometimes called "ghost of the forest" because their white, patchy bark contrasts with the darkness of the understory.

Walnut: several species (*Juglans* spp.)

Various walnuts are grown in Oregon, but the two most common are black walnut and English walnut. Sometimes two or more species are grafted together to enhance nut production. Large, pinnately compound leaves, large, hard-shelled nuts, and twigs with chambered or segmented piths are all distinctive walnut characteristics.

Black walnut (*Juglans nigra*): develops an immense, rounded head and may grow to 150 feet tall. It is easy to recognize by its huge, pinnately compound leaves (up to 24 inches long with 15 to 20 leaflets), and its hard, deeply grooved nut. Leaves and nuts both have distinctive, penetrating odors. From the hard, thick-shelled black walnut, nut meats can be extracted (with great difficulty) to furnish a delicious flavoring for ice cream, candies, and bakery products. The shells are so hard that they're sometimes added to rubber tires and asphalt to make them last longer. Limbs are larger, darker, and rougher than those of other walnuts.

English Walnut *(Juglans regia)*: the nuts are smoother and have thinner shells than those of black walnut. In addition, their leaves have fewer (generally five to seven) and much larger leaflets than black walnut. But the twig piths are still chambered. This species actually originated in Asia rather than England but was distributed and popularized by the English several centuries ago. Leaves, twigs, and fruit hulls have a strong odor and easily can stain your hands brown.

Willow: many species *(Salix* spp.)

Many willows have been introduced into Oregon for ornamental purposes. Only two will be described here.

Weeping willow *(Salix babylonica)*: best known for its dense, heavily drooping branches. Densely branched, 30 to 40 feet tall, it presents an attractive winter design. Voracious roots reach far to foul up drains. Ropes and baskets from willow slips must have been among the earliest known manufactured articles of primitive people. Originally from China, it's now widely planted.

Golden willow *(Salix alba* var. *vitellina)*: less drooping, less dense, and less invasive than weeping willow. Bright orange branches make it attractive in winter. Widely adaptable to soil and moisture conditions, it's frequently seen in eastern Oregon, where it can be used in windbreaks.

Yellow-poplar *(Liriodendron tulipifera)*

Unless damaged by snow and ice, yellow-poplar grows straight and tall, like a conifer. You can recognize it from its unusual, squarish leaves that are 3 to 8 inches long, by "duckbill" shaped buds, and by distinctive, conelike fruits that fall apart one samara at a time. Fascinating, tulip-shaped flowers give this large and likable tree its other common name, tulip-poplar. But because the flowers are greenish-yellow and blend with the leaves, they're not always noticed. The hyphen in the common name tells us this is not a true poplar *(Populus* spp.)

Oregon's Forests

R. Duddles, A. Campbell, and L. Torres

Oregon is one of our most diverse states—regardless of whether we consider its geography, its climate, its people, or its forests. Its environment ranges from cool, wet coastal lands to towering, snow-capped mountains to hot, parched deserts. Forests occupy nearly half of Oregon's total land base—almost 30 million acres. They include majestic stands of Douglas-fir and western hemlock in the Coast and Cascade ranges, snow-stunted spruce and fir forests near timberline, and open, parklike stands of pine and juniper east of the Cascades.

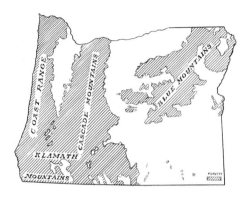

But it was not always so. In the distant past—before Oregon became a state, before people first roamed the continent, even before the mountains were formed, Oregon's forests were radically different from those we see today.

From Tree Ferns to Towering Giants

Four hundred million years ago, Oregon, like much of North America, was a warm and swampy place. Giant tree ferns and horsetails lined the swamps and probably formed our first "forests." Although they reached great size, these ferns and horsetails were not true trees—their stems were not woody, and they did not produce annual rings. About 200 million years ago, the first primitive trees—conifers, ginkos, and cycads—began to develop. They probably grew on large islands within vast inland seas.

When the extensive chain of mountains now called the Rockies began to form about 70 million years ago, the North American west began a slow drying-out process that stimulated the development of land plants. Oregon's climate and forests became subtropical in nature, dominated by trees such as palms, figs, laurels, avocados, cinnamon, and dawn-redwood, a primitive conifer now native only to China.

Over time, these subtropical plants gradually disappeared from Oregon, and our forests began to resemble those that now grow in the eastern half of North America—a mixture of maples, oaks, basswoods, elms, and sycamores, as well as a host of conifers that now grow only in the Far East.

About 13 million years ago, the Cascade Mountains and the Coast Range began to rise from the swampy sea, dramatically changing the climate of Oregon. Annual rainfall was drastically reduced east of the Cascades. Subtropical and warm-temperature trees disappeared. The survivors were trees that could tolerate cold winters and prolonged drought, such as aspens, spruces, and pines. In the western, more temperate side of the state, willows, cottonwoods, cherries, and maples flourished. By about 1 million years ago, the forests began to resemble those of today.

Then came the ice. Massive glaciers pushed down from the north and also from the valleys emanating from the Cascades and other mountain ranges. Their effect on the land was profound. These moving rivers of ice completely destroyed entire forests. Most of Oregon's forests are still recovering from the last glacial period, which ended almost 10,000 years ago.

Through time, prolonged dryness became a dominant part of Oregon's weather pattern. Along with recurring days of summer drought, wildfire emerged as a significant factor in the evolution of our forests. The severity and frequency of these fires has had a dramatic effect on the forests we see today. Huge, high-intensity fires that burned 400 to 600 years ago initiated growth of the vast Douglas-fir and western hemlock forests that cover so much of western Oregon today. Moderately intense fires played a role in the healthy growth of mixed evergreen forests composed of Douglas-fir, true fir, and a variety of broadleaved evergreen trees in southwestern Oregon. Low-intensity fires greatly contributed to the development of mixed conifer and ponderosa pine forests in eastern Oregon, as well as oak and madrone woodlands on the west side.

Such a rich and eventful past has led to an amazing diversity in Oregon's forests. The Cascade Mountains separate the lush forests of western Oregon from the high desert and dry forests of the eastern part of the state. In addition, the Siskiyou Mountains of southwestern Oregon separate the cool, humid forests of northwestern Oregon from the warmer, drier forests of California. While many broadleaved trees and shrubs are found throughout Oregon, the forests in all three regions of the state are dominated by conifers.

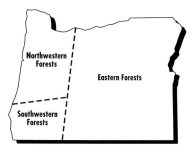

The forests of northwestern Oregon are dominated by majestic stands of Douglas-fir and western hemlock. This is the home of cathedral-like, old-growth forests that stretch nearly 300 feet into the sky and sometimes reach 800 years old. It's also the home of some of the most productive forests in the entire world, planted and managed stands of second-growth Douglas-fir. Near the coast, where rainfall is higher and dense fogs cool the summer heat, Douglas-fir gives way to a dense mixture of western hemlock, Sitka spruce, and western redcedar. At higher elevations, several species of true fir and pine often join the mix of Douglas-fir and hemlock.

The forests of eastern Oregon are greatly influenced by terrain, elevation, and the availability of water. Open, sparsely treed juniper forests occupy many of the dry, low-lying plateaus. While important for grazing, wildlife, watersheds, and other uses, juniper forests are not important for timber production. It's ponderosa pine that is the predominant species—both visually and economically—for much of eastern Oregon. These stately trees with their distinctive, yellow-plated bark are found at mid-elevations and often were the first trees that greeted early settlers upon their arrival in Oregon. Along with Douglas-fir, ponderosa pine is one of the most economically important commercial tree species in North America. As elevation and rainfall increase, ponderosa pine gives way to a mixed conifer forest of Douglas-fir, lodgepole pine, western larch, Engelmann spruce, and a mixture of true firs.

For a number of reasons, the forests of southwestern Oregon are among the state's most diverse. The transition from a cool, wet, coastal climate to a hot, dry interior is more abrupt than in the northern part of the state. Elevation changes are greater and more dramatic. The geology and soils are very old and complex. And fire has had a greater influence in shaping the forests because of a drier climate. As a result, southwest Oregon's forests are a complex mosaic of Douglas-fir and a variety of pines, false cedars, and drought-resistant hardwoods, often growing in mixed stands.

Throughout the Cascade Range and the mountains of eastern Oregon, the highest elevations support subalpine vegetation. Tree species include subalpine fir, mountain hemlock, whitebark pine, and lodgepole pine. While of little commercial value for timber, subalpine forests provide some of our most breathtaking scenery and our most spectacular recreational opportunities. For this reason, much of the subalpine forest has been permanently retained for scenic purposes in parks and wilderness areas.

People and Trees—An Inseparable Bond

Ask Oregonians what trees mean to them and you'll receive many different answers. Trees are a part of our heritage. They are a part of our lives. They have an almost spiritual importance for Oregonians.

Oregon is unique because of its beautiful, diverse, and productive forests. Whether they're providing shady relief in our urban areas, safe refuge for wildlife, or a valuable source of wood products, trees play an important role every day in our lives. That's especially true in Oregon, where trees grow so easily and in such abundance.

Economically, trees provide a significant source of employment and revenue to Oregonians. A large number of the state's workers are employed in the forest products industry. A major source of Oregon's private and public employment comes directly or indirectly from the wood products industry.

Local governments and schools in Oregon depend heavily on revenues from timber harvested from private and public lands. Of Oregon's 36 counties, many depend significantly on timber-related revenues for general services such as public health, safety, and roads.

Public values regarding our forests have changed rapidly in recent years. Much of the change results from significant urban growth throughout Oregon. While the population has changed, so has the public's views on the importance of trees. Forest products and jobs remain important cornerstones of our economy. However, an ever-increasing urban population looks to forests more for recreation, viewing wildlife, enjoying forested wetlands, and other forest values. A growing number of Oregonians are calling for the protection of sensitive resources such as threatened and endangered species. At the same time, a significant number of Oregonians depend heavily on timber production.

Finding a proper balance or middle ground between competing ecological and economic values will continue to challenge public and private land managers in the coming years. Decisions on many of these issues will be influenced greatly by how Oregonians feel about trees.

Oregon's forests have always been important to the people who have lived here—even from the earliest times. Northwest Indian tribes generally chose to live along the coast, where they used the bark and wood from forest trees, especially western redcedar, for tools, fuel, clothing, canoes, and plank houses. Although they valued the forests as a source of raw materials, they also valued them as a home for animals and spirits that were important to their culture.

As far back as the early 19th century, the Calapooya Indians of the Willamette Valley annually burned the tall grass of the savannas as an aid in gathering food and as a way to enhance detection of approaching enemies. In southern Oregon, local

Northwest Indians underburned low-elevation forests to improve game habitat and hunting. These fires often destroyed large stands of trees.

A refuge for wildlife

Large-scale changes began when European settlers moved across the prairies into the Oregon Territory. First came the explorers, fur trappers, adventurers—and even botanists. One such botanist was Archibald Menzies, a Scottish physician in the British Navy. In 1792, he made the first known collections of Douglas-fir (*Pseudotsuga menziesii*) and Pacific madrone (*Arbutus menziesii*). The scientific names of both trees now bear his name.

It was the Lewis and Clark Expedition (1804–1806), under the authority of President Thomas Jefferson, that pushed wide the gates to exploration and exploitation of western forest lands. Jefferson chose well in selecting Meriwether Lewis and William Clark to lead this group. Their detailed journals provided superb written descriptions of western trees. In one entry, they wrote that "the trees of larger growth are very abundant; the whole neighborhood of the coast is supplied with great quantities of excellent timber." In another, one tree was "found to be forty-two feet in circumference," and for a "distance of two hundred feet was destitute of limbs."

Another botanist scribed an unalterable mark on Oregon's forest history. Truly an adventurer, he traveled thousands of miles by foot, horseback, and canoe. He was David Douglas, son of a Scottish stonemason, and probably the most famous figure in the history of 19th-century American botany. Between 1825 and 1834, Douglas spent over 2½ years in Oregon, where he discovered the giant chinkapin and many different species of oak, maple, pine, fir, and spruce. The common name of Oregon's most abundant tree, Douglas-fir, honors this great adventurer.

The human relationship to Oregon forests changed drastically early in the 19th century with the arrival of significant numbers of white settlers. These folks' original interests were furs and farming. It wasn't long, however, before the forests and all their resources were being exploited. In the earliest stages of settlement, timber had little monetary value, but it was important to the lives of the new farmers. Houses, furniture, tools, utensils, vehicles, machinery, and heat all came from wood.

The first sawmill in Oregon was built in 1842 at the falls of the Willamette River in Oregon City. The California gold rush and explosive growth in San Francisco made lumbering Oregon's leading industry and set the stage for the Oregon we know today.

Over the years, Oregon has seen an increasing demand for forest resources other than timber. Oregon's economy is changing and maturing. The growing population is looking increasingly to forests for recreation, clean water, fish and wildlife, and other ecological values. Also, travel and tourism, dependent to a great extent on Oregon's majestic forests, play an increasing role in the state's economy. Tourism is the third-largest industry in the state and is growing in importance.

Because of the increasing demand on our forests to fill a variety of needs, caring for our forests becomes all the more important. Much of this is accomplished through a concept called stewardship. Stewardship means providing responsible, nurturing care—for a person, a family, a business, and even a forest. This caring and nurturing has allowed us to protect our forests, promote responsible forest practices, and encourage a variety of forest uses. It also helps Oregonians understand the diversity of benefits our forests offer and how our forests grow and survive.

Lewis and Clark kept detailed journals

The idea of stewardship isn't new. Most public and private forest landowners already practice the wise use of forest lands by emphasizing a variety of management practices. The principles behind stewardship allow forest landowners to manage their lands intensively not only for better timber growth and quality but also for better wild-

life and fisheries habitat, soil protection, aesthetics, and recreational opportunities.

As well as being biologically diverse, Oregon's forests have diverse patterns of ownership, which greatly affects how they're managed. More than half of Oregon's forests (57 percent) are federally owned and managed, primarily by the U.S. Forest Service and the Bureau of Land Management. These lands most often are managed for a variety of uses such as timber, grazing, wildlife, watershed, and recreation. But the national forests in Oregon also contain about 40 designated wilderness areas totaling approximately 2.3 million acres. These areas offer solitude and wilderness experiences that enrich the soul and rejuvenate the spirit. Crater Lake, noted for its azure blue water, is Oregon's only national park. The National Park Service also administers three national monuments: Oregon Caves, John Day Fossil Beds, and Fort Clatsop at the mouth of the Columbia River.

Who Manages Oregon's Forests?

(28 million acres)

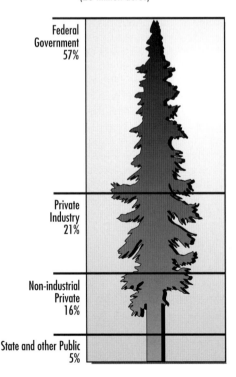

Federal Government 57%

Private Industry 21%

Non-industrial Private 16%

State and other Public 5%

Industrial owners manage about 21 percent of Oregon's forest land—primarily to produce logs and other wood products. These lands generally are among the most productive forest lands in Oregon. In the decades leading up to the 1990s, industrial forest lands accounted for nearly 40 percent of our annual timber harvest. More recently, their contribution has risen to 75 to 80 percent, due in part to declining harvests from federal lands.

Private, nonindustrial landowners own nearly 16 percent of Oregon's forests. A tremendous assortment of people fall into this category—including doctors, farmers, bankers, teachers, loggers, and lawyers. They manage their properties for a wide variety of reasons—income, wildlife habitat, livestock grazing, mushroom production, or simply to have a special place to call their own.

To understand the important role of trees in Oregon, it helps to understand the contributions of the Oregon Forest Practices Act in protecting many forest values. Passed in 1971 and revised several times since, the Forest Practices Act was the first of its kind in the nation and continues to be a national model of effectiveness.

The Forest Practices Act is designed to protect the environment during harvesting and other forest operations. A key component of the act requires that all land be reforested within 2 years of harvest. The Forest Practices Act also protects forest streams and wetlands, endangered wildlife, and designated scenic corridors. It limits clearcut size and allows for the retention of snags and green trees during forest operations. One of the act's greatest strengths is its ability to evolve over the course of time to reflect new science and the public's changing values. Throughout its history, the Forest Practices Act has changed in response to new information and as new concerns have been raised.

Currently, one of the predominant human influences on Oregon's forests is urbanization. The ever-increasing sprawl of housing developments, highways, and shopping centers continually breaks Oregon's forests into smaller and smaller fragments. Urbanization has greatly influenced the kinds of management practices that can be conducted in surrounding forests. It has fathered dramatic increases in fire hazard and in destructive forest insects and diseases. Many of these increases can be traced to physical abuses of the forest environment that, in turn, cause stress to forest trees. Soil compaction, refuse dumping, scarring trees, and improper road location are but a few examples of the human-caused stress that impairs soil structure, forested waterways, individual standing trees, and even whole forest stands.

In addition, urban growth has created new demands on forest lands for water, recreation, and clean air. Forests once harvested to provide wood products for a growing society now are being managed to filter water for drinking, to cleanse the air for breathing, to provide trails for hiking, and, in general, to soothe our spirits. In essence, the original storehouse of raw materials encountered by early American adventurers, botanists, and settlers is being reshaped to accommodate a growing nation.

Throughout history, Oregon's forests have undergone continual change. Climatic fluctuations, volcanic eruptions, fire, and exploitation by humans are just a few of the more dramatic causes. Our future—the future of Oregon's forests and the future of Oregon's people—has been and always will be linked to adaptation and change. And regardless of the unforeseen changes that will most certainly occur, forests will always play an important role in our lives.

Oregon's Big Trees

L. Torres

Big trees hold a special place in our minds and in our lore. Simply catching a glimpse of a tree that stretches 300 feet into the sky, or dwarfs the car we're riding in, often stuns us into silence.

Oregon is a special place for big trees, a place blessed with a variety of tree species that have tremendous genetic potential for growth, and blessed as well as with a climate that allows these trees to meet that potential. In fact, Oregon claims 51 champion or co-champion trees for the United States, ranking it near the top of all states as a home to big trees.

Big trees are judged on a point system developed by the American Forestry Association and are listed in its "National Register of Big Trees." A tree's total points are determined by adding together its circumference (measured 4½ feet above the ground), its height, and ¼ of its total average crown spread. Trees scoring within five points of each other are listed as co-champions. The Oregon Department of Forestry is the state coordinator for the National Register of Big Trees and maintains a list of Oregon's champions.

Oregon's largest tree is a Sitka spruce—a 206-foot-tall behemoth that grows along the coast near Seaside. Because of its tremendous diameter and crown spread, this tree earns a whopping total of 902 Big Tree Points. Despite this tremendous point total, however, it's still only the second-largest Sitka spruce in the United States.

Unlike our largest spruce, Oregon's Douglas-firs take a back seat to no one. We have national champions for both the coastal and the Rocky Mountain varieties. The coastal giant towers 329 feet above Coos County's Brummet Creek. It's taller than a 28-story building (the tallest building in Portland is 40 stories) and is more than 36 feet around—larger than two compact cars parked side by side. Its canopy, at high noon, casts a shadow the size of a swimming pool. It scores 782 points on the American Forestry Association's big-tree scale, slightly outpointing Washington's champion, which earns 762 points. Our champion Rocky Mountain Douglas-fir grows in the Ochoco National Forest, near Prineville, and tallies 454 points. It's 158 feet tall and 24 feet in circumference.

Oregon has many other champions and potential champions. If you're interested in joining the hunt for truly big trees or in obtaining a current list of Oregon's big trees, contact a local office of the Oregon Department of Forestry for additional information. You may also contact the state office in Salem (the address is below).

The following pages list many of Oregon's state and national champions. Descriptive categories include:

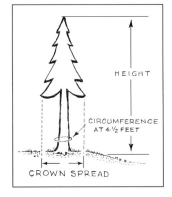

- **Stem circumference:** Distance (in inches) around the main stem at 4½ feet above the ground
- **Height:** Distance (in feet) from ground level to the top of the tree
- **Average crown spread:** Distance (in feet) as the widest tip-to-tip distance of the branches
- **Total points:** Sum of the circumference, height, and one-quarter of the crown spread
- **Status:** Tells whether the tree is the state or national champion
- **Location:** The county in which the tree can be found

Because trees are living organisms, this list will change often as the trees grow, lose their tops in storms, or die. For the newest list, contact your local office of the Oregon Department of Forestry or the state office in Salem:

Oregon Department of Forestry
2600 State Street
Salem, OR 97301

Oregon's State and National Champion Trees (and large shrubs)*

Common Name	Circum. (in)	Height (ft)	Spread (ft)	Total Points	Status	Location
Alder						
mountain alder	80	56	40	176	State	Umatilla
red alder	245	104	49	361	National	Clatsop
Sitka alder	21	30	0	51	State	Clatsop
white alder	149	92	40	251	National	Polk
Apple						
Oregon crab apple	87	39	39	136	State co-	Lincoln
Oregon crab apple	76	45	40	131	champs	Polk
Ash						
Oregon ash	284	65	68	366	National	Columbia
Aspen						
quaking aspen	120	136	44	267	State	Umatilla
Bayberry						
Pacific bayberry	48	25	28	80	State	Curry
Birch						
northwestern paper birch	46	66	30	120	National	Wallowa
water birch	113	53	46	178	National	Wallowa
Buckthorn						
cascara buckthorn	109	27	43	147	National	Lane
cascara buckthorn	99	37	50	149	co-champs	Clatsop
Buffaloberry						
silver buffaloberry	78	22	20	105	National	Malheur
California-laurel						
California-laurel	501	88	70	607	State	Curry
Catalpa						
northern catalpa	144	101	40	255	State	Washington
Ceanothus						
blueblossom	32	41	20	78	National	Curry
"Cedar"						
Alaska-cedar	303	126	52	442	State	Linn
incense-cedar	374	150	56	538	State	Josephine
Port-Orford-cedar	451	219	39	680	National	Coos
western redcedar	428	187	44	626	State	Clackamas
Cercocarpus						
birchleaf cercocarpus	44	34	29	85	National	Jackson
curlleaf cercocarpus	56	29	36	90	State	Klamath
Cherry						
bitter cherry	72	66	44	149	State	Tillamook
mazzard cherry	181	61	56	256	State	Tillamook
Chestnut						
American chestnut	233	99	95	356	State	Clackamas

*as of April 2003

Common Name	Circum. (in)	Height (ft)	Spread (ft)	Total Points	Status	Location
Chinkapin						
golden chinkapin	144	112	36	265	State	Douglas
Cottonwood						
black cottonwood	370	158	110	506	National	Marion
eastern cottonwood	282	151	113	461	State	Harney
narrowleaf cottonwood	314	79	80	413	National	Malheur
Cypress						
Baker cypress	129	129	29	265	National	Josephine
Monterey cypress	432	86	96	542	State	Curry
Dogwood						
Pacific dogwood	169	60	58	244	National	Columbia
western dogwood	32	25	36	66	State	Polk
Douglas-fir						
coastal Douglas-fir	438	329	60	782	State	Coos
Rocky Mountain Douglas-fir	316	139	56	469	National	Jefferson
Elder						
blackbead elder	39	42	30	89	National	Columbia
Pacific blue elder	105	41	32	154	State	Curry
Pacific red elder	56	27	30	91	National co-champ	Tillamook
Pacific red elder	55	24	28	86	State co-champ	Tillamook
Elm						
American elm	212	120	83	353	State	Union
Fir						
grand fir	224	194	40	428	State	Grant
noble fir	240	205	44	456	State	Linn
Shasta red fir	245	228	32	481	National	Jackson
subalpine fir	151	121	28	279	State	Union
white fir	231	175	28	413	State	Jefferson
Giant Sequoia						
giant sequoia	362	190	60	567	State	Washington
giant sequoia	392	152	70	561	co-champs	Washington
Hawthorn						
black hawthorn	36	40	32	84	State	Union
Columbia hawthorn	26	18	12	47	State	Wallowa
oneseed hawthorn	79	43	37	131	State co-	Lake
oneseed hawthorn	72	54	40	136	champs	Marion
Hazel						
California hazel	66	50	42	127	National	Lincoln
Hemlock						
mountain hemlock	258	112	40	380	State	Deschutes
western hemlock	304	195	50	512	State	Tillamook
Hickory						
shellbark hickory	80	61	60	156	State	Clackamas
Holly						
silver variegated holly	82	55	30	145	State	Tillamook

Common Name	Circum. (in)	Height (ft)	Spread (ft)	Total Points	Status	Location
Juniper						
western juniper	232	78	39	320	State	Lake
Larch						
western larch	269	103	30	380	State	Wallowa
Locust						
black locust	155	89	48	256	State	Curry
Madrone						
Pacific madrone	283	84	88	389	State	Washington
Maple						
bigleaf maple	419	101	90	543	National	Clatsop
Douglas maple	42	63	26	112	State	Hood River
silver maple	306	45	60	366	State	Baker
vine maple	56	40	34	105	National	Tillamook
Mountain-ash						
American mountain-ash	73	56	42	140	State	Lincoln
Sitka mountain-ash	19	50	18	74	National	Coos
Oak						
California black oak	338	124	115	491	National	Curry
canyon live oak	260	69	70	334	State co-	Curry
canyon live oak	255	70	44	346	champs	Curry
English oak	144	52	76	215	State	Marion
Oregon white oak	272	98	72	388	National	Douglas
shingle oak	123	97	68	237	State	Clackamas
Pine						
gray pine	142	91	46	245	State	Jackson
knobcone pine	124	99	39	233	State	Curry
lodgepole pine	128	110	48	250	State co-	Grant
lodgepole pine	145	87	52	245	champs	Deschutes
Monterey pine	208	95	74	322	National co-champ	Coos
pitch pine	155	58	17	230	State	Clatsop
ponderosa pine	342	178	45	531	State	Deschutes
Scots pine	122	77	44	210	State	Marion
shore pine	144	51	40	205	State	Curry
western white pine	249	242	35	500	State	Jackson
whitebark pine	223	72	62	311	State	Wallowa
Plum						
Chickasaw plum	130	86	48	228	National	Clatsop
garden plum	130	47	48	189	National	Multnomah
Klamath plum	42	28	19	75	National	Klamath
Poplar						
Lombardy	368	105	32	481	State	Wheeler
white	225	53	72	296	State	Clackamas
Redwood						
coast redwood	456	262	61	733	State	Curry
Russian Olive						
Russian olive	81	48	48	141	State co-	Crook
Russian olive	82	47	40	139	champs	Wasco

Common Name	Circum. (in)	Height (ft)	Spread (ft)	Total Points	Status	Location
Sagebrush						
big sagebrush	20	13	17	37	National co-champ	Jefferson
Serviceberry						
western	31	36	36	76	State	Marion
Silktassel						
wavyleaf silktassel	28	29	22	63	National	Curry
Spruce						
Brewer spruce	164	170	39	344	State	Josephine
Engelmann spruce	212	190	28	409	State	Union
Sitka spruce	673	206	93	902	National co-champ	Clatsop
Sycamore						
American sycamore	216	97	84	334	State	Wasco
Tanoak						
tanoak	275	144	60	434	National	Curry
Walnut						
black walnut	278	130	140	443	National	Multnomah
butternut	222	80	104	328	National co-champ	Lane
California walnut	243	103	110	374	State	Douglas
Willow						
arroyo willow	43	27	20	75	National	Wallowa
black willow	227	76	74	322	State	Harney
Bonpland willow	127	37	45	175	State	Klamath
Hinds willow	58	50	32	116	National	Jackson
Hooker willow	51	32	27	90	State co-champ	Clatsop
Hooker willow	65	50	39	125	National	Tillamook
Pacific willow	84	61	40	155	State	Lincoln
peachleaf willow	284	67	80	371	State	Union
Tracy willow	36	20	15	60	National	Jackson
weeping willow	239	70	60	324	State	Crook
Yellow-poplar						
tuliptree	199	121	72	338	State	Multnomah
Yew						
Pacific yew	160	70	40	240	National co-champ	Washington

Index to Trees Described in This Book

Index by Common Names

Index by Scientific Names

Recycled
Paper